MICROSTYLE

MICROSTYLE

THE ART OF WRITING LITTLE

CHRISTOPHER JOHNSON

W. W. NORTON & COMPANY

NEW YORK | LONDON

For information about permission to reproduce selections from this book,
write to Permissions, W. W. Norton & Company, Inc.,
500 Fifth Avenue, New York, NY 10110

For information about special discounts for bulk purchases,
please contact W. W. Norton Special Sales at
specialsales@wwnorton.com or 800-233-4830

Manufacturing by Courier Westford
Book design by Brooke Koven
Production manager: Devon Zahn

Library of Congress Cataloging-in-Publication Data

Johnson, Christopher, 1963 Oct. 12–
Microstyle : the art of writing little / Christopher Johnson. — 1st ed.
p. cm.
Includes index.
ISBN 978-0-393-07740-7 (hardcover)
1. English language—Style. 2. English language—Rhetoric. I. Title.
PE1421.J63 2011
808'.042—dc22

2011007712

W. W. Norton & Company, Inc.
500 Fifth Avenue, New York, N.Y. 10110
www.wwnorton.com

W. W. Norton & Company Ltd.
Castle House, 75/76 Wells Street, London W1T 3QT

1 2 3 4 5 6 7 8 9 0

For Jordanna, Tobias, and Finn

CONTENTS

MICROSTYLE

INTRODUCTION

This is the age of the Incredible Shrinking Message. Some of the most important verbal messages we encounter are also the shortest. Headlines, titles, brand names, domain names, sound bites, slogans, taglines, catchphrases, email subject lines, text messages, elevator pitches, bullet points, tweets, and Facebook status updates are a few examples. While there are plenty of style guides to consult for writing advice, from old fogies like Strunk and White's *Elements of Style* to young hipsters like Constance Hale's *Sin & Syntax*, they don't help much with little messages like these.

Messages of just a word, a phrase, or a short sentence or two—*micromessages*—lean heavily on every word and live or die by the tiniest stylistic choices. Micromessages depend not on the elements of style but on the *atoms* of style. They require *microstyle*.

Microstyle has been the secret knowledge of poets, copywriters, brand namers, political speechwriters, and other professional verbal miniaturists. Until now. You hold in your hands the first microstyle guide. Do you need to coin a new word? Come up with a short, available domain name? Capture the essence of your organization in three words? Then help is right here in these pages.

Microstyle is a guide to verbal strategies that make very short messages effective, interesting, and memorable.

But this isn't a typical style guide. Style guides as we know them are a product of a different time—a time when most people who wrote on a daily basis were professional writers or students. For the rest of us, writing was more of a special occasion. Style guides focus on things *not* to do. They urge us to avoid common mistakes of spelling and usage, jettison clichés and jargon, and break bad grammatical habits. Those books are useful, but they're essentially negative, because they play on our insecurities. Those books are part of a tradition that I call Big Style. But I'll get to that in a moment.

Like dictionaries, style guides will stick around. This book is something a little different. I like to think of it as a field guide. A style guide gives you rules to follow. A field guide is something you take out into the world with you. It can be practical—you might use it to decide which berries or mushrooms to eat—but it can also enhance your understanding and appreciation of what you see around you. So think of this as a field guide to everyday verbal ingenuity. It can help you survive in the verbal wilderness, but it can also help you explore and enjoy. And just to stretch the analogy a little further, words and phrases bear some resemblance to plants and animals. They're adapted to their natural environments, they're strange and beautiful, and they're sometimes dangerous.

Microstyle is really about language at play—even when it's used at work. You use it when you come up with a business name—or a baby name—that "has a nice ring to it." You use it when you try to make a headline or title or sign "catchy." You even use it when you think of something clever and funny to say at a party. And of course, you use it on Twitter, if you're a part of that world. Microstyle is the natural expression of verbal art and verbal playfulness. It's what makes every one of us a poet.

Is microstyle just regular old style applied to short messages? No, not really. Think about it this way: if extended prose writing is like painting or illustration, microstyle is like graphic design. It employs a subset of the techniques used in the more detailed arts, and because it serves different ends, it involves techniques and conventions of its own.

Let's flesh out that analogy a little. First, only certain aspects of style can be realized in very short messages. Paragraph structure, for example, doesn't come into play. Second, and more important, very short messages tend to serve different purposes and therefore involve different challenges. Some aspects of style in longer writing are intended to maintain cohesiveness and hold a reader's sustained attention. Microstyle is about grabbing that attention for a moment and communicating something quickly. Economy of expression is all-important. Many micromessages, such as brand names and sound bites, are also designed to be remembered and repeated verbatim.

Microstyle isn't new. Science fiction author William Gibson once observed that "the future is already here—it's just unevenly distributed." Our future—the era of the micromessage—has been here for decades, concentrated in areas of life where verbal messages compete fiercely for attention. Some quintessentially American popular art forms, such as the pop song lyric and the one-liner, are expert expressions of microstyle. There's one place where microstyle has really been honed, and the analogy to graphic design should give you a hint: advertising. Graphic design and copywriting, which is perhaps the most highly advanced form of microstyle, grew up together in the print ad, as developed by the creative team—an artist and a wordsmith working together to come up with a creative ad concept.

So there's really nothing new about microstyle. We've all been spectators of the sport for a long time. What's new is that everyone's getting into the game. The need and ability to capture instant attention are rapidly spreading to new people and new contexts and becoming the norm for daily discourse. It's no longer just specialists who need to master the art of the miniature message. It's anyone who names a website, thinks of a title for a blog post, makes a comment in an online forum, updates Facebook status, or uses Twitter to publish miscellaneous thoughts—that is, just about everyone who actively participates in web culture. It's also anyone who puts together a PowerPoint presentation, writes a personal ad, or crafts an attention-getting résumé—that is, just about everyone else.

In this book I observe microstyle in the wild, drawing on my training in linguistics and my experience as a naming and verbal branding consultant, and reveal its secret life. In the chapters that follow I freely grab examples from here and there, disregarding message categories and chronology in the interest of stylistic commonality. The "rules" discussed in this book are not limited to any particular kind of message or context; they're linguistic techniques that can be used in all kinds of miniature messages. We'll see that effective messages rely on the same techniques again and again. Think of them as tools, not rules.

WHY SHORT MESSAGES?

Daily verbal life has come to be dominated by micromessages, not because, as some commentators suggest, we're suffering from a mass onset of attention deficit disorder. It's not a sign of cultural decline. It's simple economics. Well, not quite. It's metaphorical economics. It's the verbal attention economy.

In their book *The Attention Economy*, Thomas H. Davenport and John C. Beck argue that capital, labor, knowledge, computational resources, and most important, information are all plentiful, and that human attention is now the scarce resource we all compete for. The attention economy affects verbal communication. When we consume verbal messages, we scan, skim, and screen, trying to reserve our precious attention for the ones that deserve it. When we produce verbal messages, we struggle to get them noticed. This dynamic between reader and writer favors a verbal style that's catchy and fragmented.

The attention economy is a result of the information revolution that the web and social media have made possible. Anyone with a web connection has access to an unimaginable sea of documents, databases, images, videos, and audio recordings—"information overload" already seems like a quaint way to describe this situation. Much has been said about the demands that all this information places on our beleaguered attention. Most of the talk has been about the experience of filtering and consuming information, regardless of medium. The poster child for this social problem is the pasty, harried yet lethargic web geek who watches YouTube clips, downloads MP3s, peruses blogs, and obsessively checks email while "working."

This generic tale of information overload is old hat. But a more interesting story—about how the attention economy affects our verbal life—has yet to be told. Language plays a uniquely intimate role in our thoughts and our relationships. When our experience of language changes—and it *has* changed—we're affected deeply. Most significant, we're all producers as well as consumers of verbal culture. More than any other mode of communication, language makes us experience the attention economy as seekers of others' attention, not just guardians of our own.

When the verbal attention economy *is* discussed, it's often blamed for declining reading habits and the loss of literacy. Nicholas Carr, for example, argues in his book *The Shallows* that the web, with its built-in distractions, is eroding our ability to follow extended arguments and narratives. Several other books focus on the dark side of the web revolution, including David Slayden and Rita Kirk Whillock's *Soundbite Culture: The Death of Discourse in a Wired World*; Mark Bauerlein's *The Dumbest Generation: How the Digital Age Stupefies Young Americans and Jeopardizes Our Future (Or, Don't Trust Anyone under 30)*; and Maggie Jackson's *Distracted: The Erosion of Attention and the Coming Dark Age.*

Death of discourse? Dumbest generation? Coming dark age? There's a gloomy little trio of sound bites for you. But wait, here come the cheerleaders for the future! They sing the virtues of digital technology in books like Steven Johnson's *Everything Bad Is Good for You* and Marc Prensky's *Don't Bother Me Mom—I'm Learning!* and articles like Larissa MacFarquhar's "Who Cares If Johnny Can't Read? The Value of Books Is Overstated." Things aren't just OK—they're better than ever!

People get worked up about the pros and cons of the digital age. Part of the apparent polarization, however, comes from the need to give books provocative titles that will capture readers' attention. Overstating claims to push people's buttons is a classic microstyle technique (see Chapter 4). If you use a hyperbolic yet jauntily alliterating phrase like *The Death of Discourse* in the subtitle of your book, you're participating in sound-bite culture, even if you criticize that culture inside the book.

When thinking about a change like the one our verbal culture is undergoing, it's tempting to pick a side, pro or con, and yell as loudly as you can. We can do better than that. First let's recognize that where verbal life is concerned, all the focus on technology per se is misplaced. The technology of social media simply enables a new dynamic of communication, and that's the true cause of our disorientation. The web removes economic, editorial, and temporal barriers to mass publication and distribution, creating a landscape of verbal messages that's competitive in the extreme. It amplifies an unprecedented multitude of voices. As social media observer Clay Shirky argues in *Here Comes Everybody*, the distinction between broadcast communication and simple one-to-one communication is breaking down. But when everyone is talking, no one has much time to listen. When you do stop to listen, there are so many voices that it's hard to pick a single one.

That, in a nutshell, is the verbal attention economy. As Carr and others have observed, it changes our experience of reading. On the web we scan, skim, and click around trying to make sure we don't waste our attention on things that don't deserve it. This is the verbal side of the dilemma we now face as consumers of all kinds of information.

The focus on reading, however, threatens to eclipse what may be an even more important change: the seismic shift in the way we write. The experience of writing on the web—blog posts, comments in discussion forums, even email messages to busy colleagues and friends—often requires us to be brief and attention-getting so that we won't be lost in the noise. Whatever we conclude from the broader critique of web culture, these are real challenges that many of us now face every day. And for many of us, they're *new* challenges.

We all need to think pragmatically about communication, to understand what reaches us and how we can reach others. That's not just practical; it's also a way to be culturally engaged, to notice and appreciate the verbal ingenuity that's all around us. In medieval universities, the ancient art of rhetoric—the study of effective communication—was one of the cornerstones of the original liberal arts education. We need to bring back rhetoric. Well, almost. Ancient rhetoric was based on a kind of public oratory that few of us engage in anymore. We need a rhetoric for the web age—a rhetoric of the micromessage.

A MICROHISTORY OF MICROSTYLE

Microstyle has its roots in simple conversation. A micromessage, which takes at most a few seconds to hear or read, is about the length of an average conversational turn, and when people talk face-to-face, they often strive to grab attention or be clever. Memorable bits of conversation enter our oral tradition as proverbs, aphorisms, and idioms.

The story of microstyle really got started, however, with the development of mass media in the nineteenth century. Mass media created all the conditions that shape microstyle today—most notably, the mass dissemination of words and competition for readers or listeners. The function of microstyle is to get messages noticed, remembered, and passed along. Brevity is just a minimal requirement. Prominent figures in the history of microstyle include people like Oscar Wilde, a modern-style media hound who was known as much for his witty epigrams as for his more standard literary output. One of his best-known quotes is "The only thing worse than being talked about is not being talked about." He also wrote, "If you wish for reputation and fame in the world, take every opportunity of advertising yourself."

Zipping across the Atlantic and into the twentieth century, we come to the Algonquin Round Table, a regular meeting of writers and other media types where witticisms were tested and often published the next day in participants' newspaper columns—especially Franklin Pierce Adams's "The Conning Tower," which ran in the *New York Tribune* and other New York papers from 1913 to 1941. Dorothy Parker, another literary figure known for her succinct wit, built her reputation largely by lunching at the Algonquin and making wisecracks. One of her better-known quips answered someone's challenge to use the word *horticulture* in a sentence: "You can lead a whore to culture, but you can't make her think." Offensive, perhaps; contrived, no doubt; but brilliant all the same.

Today's social media enable anyone to be Dorothy Parker. You don't have to live in New York and lunch every day with important people from the publishing world. Tim O'Reilly, the founder and CEO of O'Reilly Media, made the following observation in his blog: "Twitter, with its 140 character limit . . . is a breeding ground for the rebirth of repartee and of the aphorism and epigram." And let's not forget Facebook, LinkedIn, and other services that enable short updates.

The popularization of microstyle is part of a larger cultural phenomenon. We have a collective obsession with brevity in all media. In March 2007, *Wired* magazine called it "snack culture." Some theater festivals feature plays only a few minutes long. Short YouTube video clips have become a popular form of entertainment. A number of short speaking formats have become popular. The software developer Jason Dominus created the five-minute "lightning talk" format to get his colleagues to be more succinct. Architects Astrid Klein and Mark Dytham created the Pecha Kucha presentation format for designers, allowing twenty slides that advance automatically every twenty seconds. Brady Forrest and Bre Pettis of O'Reilly Media brought this format to the broader world with their Ignite talks, which started in Seattle and have spread worldwide. The Ignite format allows speakers five minutes each to teach the audience something. The pitch-perfect slogan for Ignite is ENLIGHTEN US, BUT MAKE IT QUICK.

On the web, people have taken a special interest in short literary forms. *Smith Magazine* has popularized the six-word story in recent years by soliciting and publishing "six-word memoirs." The inspiration for the six-word form comes from the following story, which is commonly attributed to Ernest Hemingway, though no one seems to know whether he really wrote it:

For sale: baby shoes, never used.

Snopes.com, a website that documents and investigates rumors and urban legends, suggests that the story was first made public in *Papa*, a play about Hemingway written by John de Groot, that debuted in 1996.

All these forms are about *expressive economy*, a basic design principle that's not limited to verbal messages. Maximizing the communicative power of few and simple elements was an important aim of modernism in all the arts. Cubist painters created landscapes and portraits from geometric shapes. Picasso's drawings tried to capture the human figure with a few simple lines. William Carlos Williams wrote poems, such as "The Red Wheelbarrow," using few and simple words and spare images.

CUTE CURMUDGEONS

This book is meant to bridge a gap between the way we use language and the way we talk about it. Since 2007 I've written a blog called The Name Inspector, about names, naming, and language, and I've run my own naming and verbal branding consultancy. My contacts with readers and clients have taught me that there's not only a practical need for help with naming and other verbal branding issues, but also a hunger for a different kind of popular discourse about language. Writing about language tends to fall into one of two categories: either it focuses on the arcane, exploring the quirky corners of our vocabulary and the obscure etymological origins of words, or it's overtly prescriptive, telling us about the right and wrong of grammar and usage. Prescriptive writing about language is what the market demands, because many people think about language only when they're worried about getting it wrong.

They view language as a source of potential embarrassment rather than pleasure.

Many people who enjoy language feel seduced by pop prescriptivists to identify with a persona that I'll call the Cute Curmudgeon. The Cute Curmudgeon half-jokingly expresses great consternation toward the world for not properly understanding and appreciating grammar and usage. A favorite trope is to identify a common mistake, such as confusing the contraction *it's* and the possessive form *its*, and make a humorously extreme statement about the personal offense it causes.

If there's one person who has really corralled the cult of the Cute Curmudgeon, it's Lynne Truss, author of *Eats, Shoots & Leaves*. Through the sheer charm of her prose, she managed to turn a book subtitled *The Zero Tolerance Approach to Punctuation*—punctuation, for god's sake!—into an international best seller. Some editions contain stickers that readers can use to add missing commas and apostrophes to signs.

Mignon Fogarty, a.k.a. Grammar Girl, might be the cutest curmudgeon of all. Her first name even means 'cute' in French! But she seems to have become popular by *not* acting like a curmudgeon. She's a prescriptivist who never sounds like she's judging people. Rather, she sounds like she's helping people avoid embarrassment. She's a kind, smart friend who gives grammar advice cheerfully and discreetly. Nevertheless, it seems to be fear of embarrassment, and not linguistic curiosity, that leads people to her podcasts and books.

I'm not completely against cute curmudgeonry. It's fine as long as it contributes to our understanding of language. For example, prescriptivists tend to favor enforcing distinctions in usage, such as the one between *less* and *fewer*. A long-standing argument holds that *less* should be reserved for measurable substances (whether tangible or abstract) and only *fewer* should be used with countable objects. Fine by me! I like nuances of meaning and usage. Learning this rule helps people notice the interesting and important distinction between mass nouns and count nouns.

Unfortunately, many prescriptive rules are ridiculous—for example, the ones prohibiting "split infinitives" and sentence-final prepositions—and prescriptivism has enjoyed an undue influence on our verbal culture. If you meet someone who claims to "love grammar," chances are they mean they love "correct" grammar and enjoy pointing out other people's mistakes. That's the sorry state of linguistic discourse in the United States, and it breaks linguists' hearts. If you tell someone you're a linguist, the most likely response—after "How many languages do you speak?"—is "I guess I'd better watch my grammar then." These answers reveal both a lack of understanding of linguistic issues and a deep insecurity about language. Linguists are, quite simply, specialists who take a scientific interest in language. They want to know how language works, and they're not interested in judging you.

Prescriptive rules are among the least interesting things about language. They remind me of a scene from the Disney/Pixar animated film *Ratatouille*, about Remy, a gifted rat who longs to be a gourmet chef. His father, who neither understands nor appreciates his aspirations, puts him to work as the rat colony's official poison sniffer. Though Remy has an uncanny ability to identify subtle ingredients in complex dishes, his job is to detect the mere presence or absence of poison in scraps of scavenged food. His work helps the rat colony but provides none of the joy he gets from cooking.

Prescriptivists are linguistic poison sniffers. They pay little attention to what makes language delicious. I want to remedy that. I believe that people could genuinely love language more if they shifted their focus from judgment and insecurity to curiosity and appreciation. We do interesting things when we use language, whether or not we're being "correct," and we should all be able to relish and discuss those things without fear of embarrassment.

BIG STYLE

There is no apostrophe in "Diners Club" but who cares?
What is this, 1953?
— @FakeAPStylebook, Twitter, April 2, 2010

Our culture conflates grammar and style with correctness because, until recently, most people wrote only when they were being formally evaluated: in school, in cover letters for job applications, and perhaps at work. Imagine (or remember!) a time before Twitter, before Facebook, before blogs, before online chat, before email. Unless you were a published author, an avid diarist, or an unusually prolific letter writer, you probably didn't write much outside those formal contexts.

It's not hard to see how Big Style got a grip on the public imagination. We like to believe that we live in a meritocracy, and that professional opportunity is based on ability. Our educational system increasingly focuses on sorting students according to their success at performing academic tasks. Standardized testing abounds, and the written essay has become a showcase for intellectual abilities that aren't revealed by multiple-choice exams. Prescriptive rules of grammar and usage provide a fairly objective way for teachers to evaluate student writing, and give comfort to students who want to understand how to perform the writing task correctly.

For journalists, technical writers, and other writing professionals whose aims aren't primarily artistic, standardization performs the same function that it does for restaurant chains: it eliminates unpleasant surprises that can be caused by strong flavors. Language is a domain in which preferences and social prejudices are strongly felt, and the use of an unexpectedly casual register or a regionally specific or "substandard" usage can often seem pungent. Journalists learn to write in a style that's palatable to everyone (just as newscasters learn to neutralize their regionally specific accents). For amateur writers, standardization and style guides offer relief from anxiety by telling us how the experts do it.

Things are different now. We all have the means, motive, and opportunity to create media content. The means, of course, is the web—and more specifically, social media tools and platforms such as blogs, wikis, forums, YouTube, Flickr, and Twitter. The opportunity is the computer on your lap or the phone in your pocket. And the motive? There are many—curiosity, self-expression, the desire to be part of a community. But there's an especially important one fostered by social changes accompanying the growth of the web and social media. Those changes are affecting the relation between people and work.

We're a "Free Agent Nation," an idea that Daniel H. Pink wrote about for *Fast Company* magazine in 1997. Changes in employment practices have eliminated the kind of job security that people experienced in the middle of the twentieth century, especially in large corporations. Attitudes toward employment have changed as well, as people seek to work for companies that share their values. People change jobs, and even careers, far more often than they used to. This mobility makes networking essential. It encourages people to cultivate résumés instead of climbing corporate ladders, and it creates a constant need for them to sell themselves, to engage in what's sometimes called "personal branding."

WE'RE ALL MAD MEN NOW

The television drama *Mad Men*, which depicts a fictional Madison Avenue ad agency of the 1960s called Sterling Cooper, clearly struck a chord with the web-savvy set at the start of the twenty-first century. In 2008, during the show's second season, it became a fad among users of Twitter to replace their avatars—the little pictures that appear next to the messages they publish on the service—with cartoon *Mad Men*–era versions of themselves. That same year, the *New York Times Magazine* ran a cover story titled "Mad Men Has Its Moment." Certainly there were many reasons to like the show, including the meticulous period dress and the near-ethnographic depiction of outdated attitudes about sex, gender roles, race, ethnicity, the workplace, child rearing, and the environment. People liked to watch *Mad Men* and think, "Look how much we've changed!"

I believe a big part of the show's appeal also lies in the advertising industry itself, and more specifically, in the protagonist Don Draper, the creative director at Sterling Cooper. Despite being very much of his time and place, Draper is in some ways the show's most contemporary character. Part of the reason is his work. He's an idea guy and a word guy of a very particular type. He runs creative meetings and often ends them by coming up with the perfect phrase for an ad campaign (or recognizing when a colleague has come up with the perfect phrase). Sometimes he's shown lying in bed jotting phrases down on a matchbook, a napkin, a newspaper.

While many aspects of life in the agency—the rigid gender roles, three-martini lunches, and debauched boys' nights out with prospective clients—seem to be from a time long ago, Don Draper's work seems of the moment. We can all relate to his search for the perfect concept and the perfect phrase to express it. He's one of us. Or, we're one of him.

SEXY ICE CUBES

The classic critical look at the ad business from the *Mad Men* era was Vance Packard's *The Hidden Persuaders*, published in 1957. Packard's book examined the motivational research used in advertising and political campaigns of the 1950s and presented a suspicious view of advertising that resonated with the public. Packard warned about the "depth approach" to persuasion, the product of a collaboration between "motivational analysts" (psychologists and other social scientists who tried to understand people's subconscious reasons for making purchasing decisions) and "symbol manipulators" (the copywriters, graphic designers, and others who applied that knowledge to create ads and other persuasive messages). Although Packard did not condemn the advertising industry as a whole, he expressed concern that the depth approach was an affront to human dignity and freedom, comparing it to George Orwell's Big Brother.

This was the era of Big Style, and most people related to media content as consumer to product: experts produced media content, and everyone else ate it up. Not surprisingly, this "expert" culture gave media content a certain mystery that made it both glamorous and threatening. Advertising in particular, created by businesses with ulterior motives to influence our behavior, stirred anxiety and aroused suspicion. What were those wizards doing, pulling all those secret levers and pushing those buttons? There were the shady agents of persuasion doing their work behind closed doors, and then there were the innocent masses being manipulated and taken advantage of.

By 1980 *The Hidden Persuaders* had sold over a million and a half copies. It helped create a market for sensationalist books such as Wilson Bryan Key's *Subliminal Seduction* (1974), which argued that advertisers were embedding sexual words and images in seemingly innocent photos and illustrations. The cover photo shows a glass full of ice cubes that supposedly contain such images. Inside the book there's another photo of ice cubes, next to a bottle of Gilbey's gin, in which the word *sex* is claimed to be subtly visible. (I see the *S* and the *E*, but the *X* is a stretch.) Key saw the word *sex* hidden everywhere; the phrase "hidden

SEXes" riddles his book. In one of his most outlandish "analyses," Key claimed that a *Playboy* centerfold was surrounded by hidden SEXes. Apparently he thought that an image of a beautiful nude woman kneeling and bending over provocatively wasn't truly titillating until it was tarted up by the awesome power of hidden words.

There's no evidence that subliminal advertising was ever as prevalent as Key and others claimed, and subsequent research has suggested that it's not especially effective anyway. In 1992 two psychologists from UC Santa Cruz, Anthony Pratkanis and Elliot Aronson, argued in their book *Age of Propaganda* that their thorough survey of relevant research showed no significant effect of subliminal messages on behavior.

That's not to say that advertisers and marketers don't want to manipulate people. They do. And just as Packard argued, they hire psychologists and social scientists to help them invent new ways to do it. The power attributed to advertising, however, in Packard's (and especially Key's) critique is beginning to seem dated. Today the idea that someone might try to sell gin by half-hiding the word *sex* in some ice cubes seems quaint. The idea that the persuasive power of advertising was somehow hidden also seems dated. Usually it's right there in your face. Advertisers use sex to sell? Duh. Advertisers appeal to our deepest desires and insecurities? Well, yeah. The hysteria about subliminal advertising seems to have come from a different time, a time when people believed that words and images, in the hands of the evil wizards of mind control, had awesome and mysterious powers.

Today social media are causing a fundamental shift in public attitudes toward persuasion. It's a shift in perspective similar to the one that takes place when a worker becomes a manager, or a student becomes a teacher. Our suspicion of The Man, and in particular, The Mad Man, is based on a caricature. In the age of mass media, we were passive consumers of persuasive messages and bound to be wary of the people and organizations that created them. But now the world is more entrepreneurial. We have the opportunity to talk back to companies and even to *be* companies. An individual blogger can start a mini media empire. An individual software developer can release applications directly to the public. Collectors and artisans have their own web stores on eBay and Etsy. Many people now have a personal stake in branding and advertising, and that familiarity demystifies and destigmatizes those pursuits. People who aren't directly involved in micro-entrepreneurial activities probably know others who are. Branding doesn't seem so bad when it's for your husband's startup or your girlfriend's band.

The line between persuader and persuaded is becoming less like the one between labor and management and more like the one between driver and pedestrian—one we might cross over frequently in a single day. More and more people are learning what it means to try to get their messages heard by a mass audience, and more and more media messages are taking on a marketing or promotional role.

HOW WE READ NOW

In 2007, the National Endowment for the Arts released a study showing that Americans are reading less than they used to. This was a follow-up to a 2002 report that arrived at the same conclusion. One of the activities that replaces reading, according to the study, is "using the computer." You might object that one of the main reasons we "use the computer" is to read. But that sort of reading doesn't count for the NEA. In its study, reading means reading books, and more specifically, literature: novels, plays, and poems.

Social media expert Stowe Boyd wrote in his blog,

I have found myself reading less in recent years: reading in the sense of hours immersed in a book, curled up on the couch. I am reading more today, in terms of text passing through my eyes, than ever before, however. It's just time spent in the browser.

Although there's some debate as to whether we're actually reading less, no one denies that we're reading differently. In his book *The Shallows*, Nicholas Carr eloquently describes how his experience of reading has changed: "Once I was a scuba diver in the sea of words. Now I zip along the surface like a guy on a Jet Ski." Web usability expert Jakob Nielsen has carefully studied the way people read on the web. His conclusion is that we don't. What we do, he claims, is scan web pages and do "information foraging." In an article titled "How Users Read on the Web" Nielsen wrote, "Instead of spending a lot of time on a single page, users move between many pages and try to pick the most tasty segments of each."

Some argue that this new way of reading is bad for us. If it's the *only* kind of reading we do, it is, but there's an undeniable logic to it. On the web, your choice of reading material is unlimited, and quality control is often conspicuously absent. There's a 90 percent chance of drivel. If you read serendipitously—one of the great pleasures of the web—the best you can do to avoid the drivel is to scan headlines, screen as well as you can, skim articles until you're convinced you're reading something worthwhile, and click away when you realize you're not. It would be foolish not to embrace this strategy.

Consider the conditions that allow you to curl up with a book and confidently devote your full attention to it. Why are you reading this book? Chances are it was recommended to you by a trusted source: an educator, a critic, a friend. Maybe you read a review, or a bookstore displayed it prominently enough for you to notice it. Maybe you read the nice comments on the back. Quality filters helped you make your decision.

There were other filters before that. I had to submit a proposal to publishers and go through a competitive process to secure a book deal. I had to work with an editor to ensure that my manuscript made sense to someone besides me. My completed manuscript had to pass muster. A lot of work went into making sure this book would deserve your attention. On the web, most of the burden of that work has been placed on the shoulders of readers. It's no wonder we read differently there.

The new way of reading isn't just lazy or unfocused; it's *guarded*. The verbal attention economy creates reading anxiety. The sad irony is that we often waste our time clicking around because we don't want to waste our attention. We don't always give it willingly, but it can be captured.

Words and phrases can do that. They have a way of grabbing us. Have you ever found yourself using a faddish expression, buzzword, or catchphrase despite yourself? Referring to the web as the "interwebs"? Calling your home your "crib" and your car your "ride"? If so, you might have felt possessed by something outside yourself. William S. Burroughs wrote that "language is a virus," capturing the feeling we sometimes have of being possessed by, rather than possessing, language. (Of course, Burroughs also said that language was "from outer space," but that part was just crazy talk.) Linguistic expressions seem to exist outside human minds, to take up residence in them, and to be transferred from one to another, much like viruses.

To use a somewhat trendier version of this metaphor, we might say that words and phrases are "memes." For a while *meme* was a fashionable buzzword. You might say there was a *meme* meme. People were always talking about this or that meme on the web. There was the blog-tagging meme, which had bloggers writing on certain topics or making lists ("8 things you don't know about

me") and then "tagging" other bloggers to do the same, chain letter style. Any popular thing on the web that people linked to a lot
was a meme. As the word *meme* became more and more popular,
it got harder to remember why we used it rather than other perfectly good words, like *fad* or *idea*.

If anything deserves to be called a meme, it's a micromessage.
Let's return to the roots of the meme idea for a moment. In *The
Selfish Gene*, evolutionary biologist Richard Dawkins argued that
the processes of variation, inheritance, and selection, which form
the basis of Darwinian evolution, might help us understand the
nebulous and ever-changing realm of cultural phenomena. He
proposed the meme as the cultural equivalent of the gene. In biological evolution, genes carry information that determines inherit-
able traits. Mutations are changes to the information in genes that
can cause changes in traits. When a mutation leads to a new trait
that gives an organism some kind of reproductive advantage, the
mutation spreads, because the organisms that have it tend to have
lots of offspring that also carry it. Over time, the trait predominates in a population. That's how biological evolution works.

There are indeed interesting parallels between this process and
the way certain cultural phenomena spread. Ideas, phrases, songs,
fads, and other cultural practices undergo processes of mutation
(people, intentionally or accidentally, modify them) and selection (people remember and repeat some and forget or ignore others). And while they're not exactly inherited, they are passed on.
A biological theory of culture promises to tame the messy realm
of human expression and enthusiasm with science, and that, no
doubt, appeals to lots of people—especially the geeks who set the
tone for web culture.

The biological analogy goes only so far, though. Some
researchers, such as Scott Atran, director of research in anthro-
pology at the Centre Nationale de la Recherche Scientifique in
Paris, argue that culture is communication, and communication

doesn't work through exact replicas the way genetic reproduction does. Communication is based on calling to mind shared knowledge and inviting people to make inferences based on it.

But verbal fragments succeed as memes through repetition, and repetition need not depend on the precise communication of meaning. It's the form of a message that is repeated, and purely formal properties can make a message memorable. Micromessages often feature the formal traits of poetry: rhyme, alliteration, assonance, structural parallelism. These are properties of the sound and structure of language, which are much more regular and predictable than meaning, so they're more closely analogous to the kinds of information that can be encoded in genes.

That's not to say meaning isn't important in micromessages. Our responses to the meanings of words are immediate and automatic, which is one of the things that makes them so powerful.

Any well-rehearsed skill is almost like a new form of perception built upon our existing faculties. Consider driving. It involves the coordination of vision, awareness of the locations of all the controls (wheel, pedals, turn signals, rearview mirror, side mirrors, horn, defogger, etc.), tactile feedback from the wheel and the pedals, awareness of sounds from approaching vehicles, and so on. Despite its complexity, longtime drivers experience driving as a simple, natural phenomenon, and can easily do it while thinking about something else.

Language is the ultimate well-rehearsed skill. We start learning to distinguish linguistic sounds before we even leave the womb, and we start to practice making our own sounds shortly after we're born. Before long we can identify the meanings of simple words and phrases, and we usually start producing our own words around our first birthday. Our verbal practice starts early, occurs constantly after that, and never ends. We're always learning new words, new expressions, new nuances of meaning, and constantly reinforcing the ones we already know.

After all this practice, our responses to verbal stimuli are so automatic that they're almost impossible to ignore. In a famous experiment reported in 1935 by John Ridley Stroop in the *Journal of Experimental Psychology*, subjects see a series of color words printed in colored ink. The color of each word is different from the color named by that word; for example, the word *blue* might be printed in red ink. Subjects are asked to simply name the colors in which the words are printed. The task proves remarkably difficult. Most people can't ignore the verbal information they get from the printed words no matter how hard they try, and they start to read the words aloud rather than naming the colors in which they're printed. The presence of verbal information interferes with their ability to see and name the colors themselves—a phenomenon that's now known as the *Stroop effect.*

This effect shows that the detection of meaning in the face of a familiar linguistic symbol is automatic, like a perception. Words are little bundles of labeled meaning that we're all built to learn, remember, and share. They're there at the beginning of our lives, and they were there in the evolutionary environment of our ancestors. They're the original memes.

That makes the micromessage the ultimate tool for getting noticed on the cheap, so microstyle is on the front line of the battle for attention on the web. It costs next to nothing to create a verbal message, and once you do, you can distribute it just as cheaply. The computational resources needed to move short snippets of text around the web are trivial. And thanks to its role in our evolutionary history, language has another unique, and uniquely cheap, distribution channel: humans. Language doesn't require special equipment. People produce verbal culture all the time, just by having conversations. Verbal messages, as long as they're short enough, can be spread by people talking in the course of their daily lives—good old word of mouth.

HOW WE WRITE NOW

The ongoing changes in our reading habits are hugely important and interesting phenomena, but there may be an even bigger story: the way we write has changed just as much. In fact, writing has probably changed more, because it has gone from being a specialist's activity to being a normal daily activity for regular people.

Text-based communication tools, and the social media that make use of them, are driving this change. We have an unprecedented opportunity to incorporate writing into our daily lives using email, text messaging, online chat, blogs, online forums, Twitter, Facebook, and other tools and services. And they give us access to a mass audience. Or rather, they give us potential access. It's up to us to actually make people pay attention.

The cultural implications of these changes should not be underestimated. Many of us now have our fingers on keyboards all the time. That just wasn't true twenty-five years ago. Most of us write not to be evaluated, but to communicate, to entertain, to persuade, to get attention. Andrea Lunsford, a professor of English, writing, and rhetoric at Stanford University, calls this kind of writing "life writing." She thinks the online world, far from destroying literacy, is creating a renaissance of literacy driven by life writing. Clive Thompson, writing for *Wired* magazine, called it the "new literacy." Microstyle isn't "micro" just because it's about short messages. It's also about these smaller, more intimate writing contexts. When we write now, it's often to make small observations about daily life, not to develop extended arguments or narratives.

The new literacy has new rules. Or rather, it doesn't really have rules as we know them, because the rules we know are embedded in official contexts that are irrelevant to life writing. Our life writing is still evaluated, but collectively, and by peers rather than authority figures. Whatever rules emerge from this kind of peer evaluation will be less arbitrary, more flexible, and less intimidating. Making mistakes in a Big Style context can mean not getting into the college of your choice or not landing a plum job. Making a mistake in a microstyle context just means having to issue a quick correction and maybe make a little self-deprecating joke.

So writing now is more interpersonal. Except when it's not. Any snippet of language published online serves two purposes: communicating something to people, and blazing a trail through the tangle of digital signals that is the web. Before people read anything on the Internet, machines read it first. This duality is built into the web's infrastructure. A domain name like amazon. com contains a brand name and a word of English that means something to people, but it also functions as a unique address that helps route signals between a website's server and a client's browser. Blog titles, post titles, and post content can all be "optimized" for search engines through the careful use of keywords.

In fact, the whole web is built out of text. The basic Internet protocols that make the web run, like TCP/IP, were created before we had graphical web browsers, and they were based on command-line interactions that people could control with simple typewriter-like Teletype interfaces. (My elementary school classmates and I had the dubious distinction of using a Teletype machine and an old-fashioned dial-up modem—the kind that you plug the phone handset directly into—to play what was certainly one of the earliest first-person shooter games. It was The Oregon Trail. To hunt for food, we had to type "BANG" as fast as we could.)

Text has acquired even more significance on the web as Google and similar search engines have become the preferred form of web navigation. Though there are technologies for searching images, text search is the most effective and widely used type of search.

Anyone who wants to be found on the web had better provide the text to make it happen.

This situation has led to a new generation of words coined specifically for the web. The best-known examples are Web 2.0 names with strange spellings, like *Flickr* and *digg*. Tweaked words like these draw on the meaning of existing words while making it possible to secure ".com" domain names. They also serve as unambiguous keywords for search engines. Some marketing experts, such as Seth Godin, maintain that a name for a new company should be a unique word or phrase that yields no results whatsoever in Google, so that when someone searches for the name, only relevant results will appear. Hence the name of his company: Squidoo.

Some people have even tried to introduce the neologism-as-unique-keyword into normal conversation on the web. Consider the word *hoosgot*, a respelling of the phrase "who's got." It was coined by Doc Searls (senior editor for *Linux Journal* and one of the authors of *The Cluetrain Manifesto*) and David Sifry (founder of the blog directory and search engine Technorati). The Hoosgot website invites people to use the word *hoosgot* when they publish questions on their blogs or in their Twitter posts. For example, someone might write, "Hoosgot a good laptop bag for camping?" Then Hoosgot's search technology will find the questions, publish them as blog posts on the website, and invite people to provide answers as comments on those posts. Users can receive the answers as RSS feeds.

So the word *hoosgot* is three things at once: a domain name, a unique keyword that can be picked up by search engines, and a phrase of English that's used normally in sentences, though with an altered spelling. It's a word designed both for humans and for the web, and it gives us a hint about the direction our vocabulary might take in the future.

HOW WE THINK ABOUT LANGUAGE

Big Style has had a strong influence on our verbal culture. Because people tend to reflect consciously on language only when they write, Big Style set the tone for the way we think about language. Grammar, which is really just the structure of language as we all speak it, became all about being correct, about getting it right.

Big Style hasn't gone away. We still produce long, formal documents, and we still have good reasons to follow the rules when we do. And yet, Big Style seems less and less relevant to the kind of writing that most of us do every day. Our new mode of writing requires a new way of thinking about language and style. Instead of Big Style, we need microstyle—the style of short messages, removed from the context of long, formal documents and the institutions in which they're evaluated. It's "micro" both because it's about more informal, interpersonal writing and because it's about the shorter texts we create.

So, in addition to being a field guide, this book is a modest manifesto. A micromanifesto. We need to think differently about language, grammar, and style. There's an odd mismatch in contemporary culture between the way we use language and the way we think and talk about it. Everyday language use embraces creativity, pragmatism, and pleasure. Commentary about language, on the other hand, leans heavily toward the pedantic and judgmental. That's largely because it's based on the idea of Big Style, associated with formal writing tasks. Microstyle, on the other hand, is all around us every day. It's informal, adaptive, hardworking, and fun. Language belongs to all of us, and it's something we all have the opportunity to enjoy, like the natural world. Let's approach it with interest, not with anxiety. Here's my manifesto:

Pay attention to the language around you in the spirit of appreciation and curiosity.

WHAT WILL THIS BOOK DO FOR YOU?

Microstyle is all about expressive economy in language: getting a lot of idea out of a little message. The tools that I discuss directly serve the purpose of expressive economy. Ambiguity gives us two meanings for the price of one. Metaphor creates complex ideas out of simpler ones. Metonymy evokes complex situations via simple details. Sound symbolism squeezes meaning out of non-meaningful aspects of sound. These are some of the topics we'll explore in the following chapters.

The book is divided into four sections: Meaning, Sound, Structure, and Social Context. These are four basic dimensions of verbal communication. Each chapter discusses one tool that helps miniature messages grab attention, communicate instantly, stick in the mind, and roll off the tongue. Each chapter is loaded with examples of a tool used well. You'll also find examples of messages that don't work, either because they fail to use a tool or because they use it badly. Some examples pop up more than once because they use more than one tool.

WHO WROTE THIS BOOK?

My story reflects what's been happening to our verbal culture. I started college at the University of Chicago thinking I was going to be an English major. I set the typical course for would-be writers: read lots of novels and learn about narrative structure and point of view and all those literary things.

I gradually learned that I was more interested in language

on a smaller scale. I got into poetry and poetic structure. Then I took a course in anthropological linguistics taught by Michael Silverstein, a charismatic professor who taught so vigorously that he sometimes got chalk on the end of his nose while outlining his lectures on the blackboard. Silverstein assigned readings that examined short, ordinary texts from a linguistic and semiotic perspective, and I was hooked.

One linguist we read was Roman Jakobson. He did a poetic analysis of Dwight D. Eisenhower's famous political slogan I LIKE IKE that has stuck with me throughout my adult life. Phonetically, the word *like* contains the word *Ike*, and the word *Ike* contains the word *I*. As Jakobson put it, this short phrase gives us an "image of a feeling which totally envelopes its object" and shows us "the loving subject enveloped by the beloved object."

That kind of attention to the microstructure of language really excited me. It also jibed with my interest in certain basic questions about language and meaning: How do words summon such complex ideas and feelings? Why do some phrases just sound right and stick in our minds? How can we be creative when we follow linguistic convention? How do our forms of speech relate to the way we live?

I moved away from literary studies and designed an interdisciplinary program in linguistics, philosophy, and psychology to study the way meaning works in language. After I graduated, I went to UC Berkeley to get a PhD in linguistics.

When I entered grad school, Berkeley was the world center of "cognitive linguistics," an approach to language that explores its connections to our other cognitive abilities and to culture. I studied word meanings, the way they relate to larger conceptual structures and metaphors, and the way they serve as a sort of interface between concepts and grammar. I studied the way grammar, far from being a set of abstract rules, is suffused with patterns that are specific and meaningful.

While enjoying this steady diet of linguistic esoterica, I was given a rare opportunity to apply it to real paying work: a job as a namer and name analyst at Lexicon Branding. So I shuttled between the scholarly Shangri-la of Berkeley and Lexicon's office in Sausalito, where I worked part-time during many semesters of grad school and full-time during the summers.

Lexicon is one of the top naming firms in the country and, with its proximity to Silicon Valley, has made technology names a specialty. Some of Lexicon's best-known names are Pentium, PowerBook, and BlackBerry. Other Lexicon names include Zima, Swiffer, Febreze, and Dasani. I worked as a namer on a number of those projects. I also developed techniques for evaluating names and wrote countless analyses of the strengths and weaknesses of names for clients, developing a perspective on words that informs what I do now—including writing this book.

Shifting gears between the academic and commercial worlds was sometimes disconcerting. The university was a factory for weighty dissertations, and Lexicon was a little workshop where people crafted names just a handful of letters long. In grad school I was trained to write scholarly papers that explored subtle arguments and acknowledged all existing literature on a topic. At Lexicon I had to get to the point. Clients didn't want to learn about language, they wanted to build brands and sell products. It became a fun challenge to find ways to make linguistics useful, and I learned to respect the craft of creating messages in the miniature.

After finishing grad school, I got involved in the first web technology boom, developing ways to model linguistic meaning for software applications. Then I taught linguistics in the Department of Comparative Human Development at the University of Chicago. I've considered language in many contexts, including ones in which it's learned by children and modeled by computer software.

These experiences have given me a multifaceted view of language that I carry with me every day. I still write analyses of names—mostly company names—on my blog The Name Inspector. They're an excuse to write about linguistic issues for nonspecialists. I also work as a naming and verbal branding consultant, helping businesspeople use microstyle to draw attention to their companies and products and present them in the best possible light.

When I'm reading and writing, I'm hyperaware of the words and phrases I encounter and use—not in an "is it correct?" way, but in a "how does it work?" way. When I consider the fragments that make up normal verbal life, I see specimens of the diverse flora and fauna of our new verbal ecosystem. I wrote this book to share some of the things I see, to let you observe words in the wild through a linguist's eyes.

MEANING

Thinking about language is strange. We all have conscious ideas about how language works, but we also have a capacity to *use* language that's not readily accessible to conscious awareness. It's part of the inner workings of the mind, rather than one of the mind's products, and it doesn't always correspond to what we think we know about language. Psychologists sometimes call these inner workings the "cognitive unconscious." When we think about the unconscious, we tend to think about Freud and his notion of the affective unconscious, the shadowy world of implicit motives that underlie emotional life. People in psychotherapy sometimes become aware of forces in their emotional lives that they had been unaware of. They start therapy believing that they're afraid of something, and they leave understanding that what they're really afraid of is their own *response* to what they fear.

The cognitive unconscious is similar, except it involves cognitive processes such as planning and reasoning rather than emotional ones. It sounds mysterious, but when you think about it, it's really not. Think of the mind as a tool for understanding things, a kind of movie camera. It understands something by taking a picture of it, but it can't take a picture of itself at the same time. The mechanisms that allow it to work have to be behind the lens, not in front of it. Similarly, we have knowledge that enables us to use language, but it doesn't allow us to *understand* how we're using language at the same time.

That's where linguists come in. By reflecting carefully on the things people say, linguists try to understand that unconscious ability, confusingly called "knowledge," that enables people to use language. Doing that requires a shift in perspective that characterizes any scientific pursuit. To build fundamental understanding, you have to be able to ask questions about things that seem obvious. To understand gravity, Newton had to think, "I know things fall down, but why?" To really get microstyle, you're going to have to set aside what you know about language and start to think like a linguist.

So, how do you pack a lot of meaning into a little message? You don't. That's the first lesson of microstyle. A message isn't a treasure chest full of meaning. It's more like a key that opens doors. A message starts a mental journey, and meaning is the destination. A successful message sends people in the right direction but allows them to use their wits and the cues provided by context to get there. Keeping this in mind makes you think about how your message fits into a larger picture and *points to* ideas without expressing them directly. The interaction of message, mind, and context makes meaning happen.

Our casual beliefs about language sometimes make it hard to see this. We think of words as containers for meaning that we ship back and forth. We think the meaning should be easy to "get out." This way of thinking is reflected in the things we say about language. We talk about words being "full of meaning" or "empty." We talk about having trouble "getting any meaning out of" a passage or "extracting any meaning from" it. A philosopher named Michael Reddy wrote a paper about this conception of language, which he called the "conduit metaphor," and that paper in turn inspired the linguist and cognitive scientist George Lakoff to develop a theory of *conceptual metaphor*, the deeply entrenched ways in which we use metaphor to think about things (we'll return to this topic in Chapter 7).

Think about how natural the conduit metaphor is. Even our dictionaries reinforce it. They list words and give them discrete definitions. We don't, however, represent the meanings of words in our minds as discrete definitions. Word meanings are made out of concepts, and concepts aren't discrete entities. They exist in networks of interrelatedness.

NETWORKS OF ASSOCIATIONS

Meanings aren't entities that can be moved from place to place. Meanings are made out of human concepts. When we successfully communicate with other people, it's not because the words we use carry our meaning to them. Rather, the words function as clues that allow them to form concepts in their own minds and in their own ways. Those concepts just have to be similar enough to our own for the purpose at hand.

Concepts don't come neatly packaged. They arise from complex activity in our brains. One of the most influential approaches to cognitive science (the study of the mind) in recent decades has been the *neural network* approach. Neural networks are abstract models of the brain, inspired by brain physiology, that are implemented as computer programs. They consist of many "nodes," each connected to many others, forming a complex web of interrelatedness. Nodes may be "activated" and send signals to other nodes. When that happens, activation can spread through the network, from node to node. In this kind of model, concepts are typically represented not as individual nodes or as discrete symbols, but as patterns of activation. To put it simply, they're not things, they're *occurrences*.

In a neural network, an activated concept typically activates other concepts through shared features. In the case of a word meaning—a concept associated with a verbal form—the shared features might be features of sound or of meaning. A word like *pig* might activate other words that sound similar, such as *pin*; thoughts of other farm animals, such as cows; and concepts related to pigs, such as pork, ham, bacon, wallow, mud, and so forth. So, concepts exist in networks of associations.

That makes meanings more multifaceted than traditional views have recognized. A traditional way to think about meaning, heavily influenced by the philosopher Gottlob Frege, divides it into denotation and connotation. The *denotation* of a word is its informational content—not unlike a dictionary definition. Denotation is closely associated with objects that people refer to and factual statements about them. Denotation is what we would consider if we were trying to decide whether a message was true or false.

Connotation is all that fuzzy stuff that a word makes us think about that goes beyond the explicit informational content. While denotation of the word *politician* would be something like 'a person holding or running for political office,' the connotation (or connotations, since the word is often used in the plural) would involve popular beliefs and stereotypes about politicians, such as the idea that they're insincere, that they wear blue suits, that they crave power, and so on. Because denotation is associated with factual statements, it's often regarded as having an objective existence, independent of people's personal thoughts and feelings. Connotation, on the other hand, is understood to be a matter of people's subjective mental associations. It's not difficult to imagine how connotations might arise through spreading activation in a neural network model.

The distinction between denotation and connotation is fine as far as it goes—at least it recognizes that meaning has the distinctly mental dimension represented by connotation—but it doesn't go very far. If you think of meaning as a network, you see how it can go off in different directions from the same point of origin. Or, to use a different image, if meaning is an object, then it has many sides. It's not just denotation and connotation.

One field of study that provides a framework for thinking about the multifaceted nature of meaning is semiotics, the general theory of signs. Semiotics seeks to understand all things that signify, or have meaning. One of the most famous semioticians was Charles Sanders Peirce, an American logician. He strove to answer the question, "How can one thing stand for another?" His theory of signs recognized three main ways of meaning, or "modes of signification"—iconic, indexical, and symbolic. *Iconic* signification is based on what we can loosely think of as similarity. Representational paintings, drawings, maps, diagrams, and computer icons all depend on iconic representation. *Indexical* signification is based on real-world connections that can be used to identify things (the word *indexical*, like the term *index finger*, is based on the ancient Greek word meaning 'to point'). Such a connection might be forged in the moment of communication, as when a person physically points at something, or it might be based on our knowledge of the world, as when a detective uses a hair to establish someone's presence at a crime scene. What's important to remember about indexical representation is that it's characterized not by similarity but by correlations in the world—such as the correlation between wholes and their parts, or between causes and their effects—that create mental associations. Finally, *symbolic* signification is based on social conventions. A word, for example, means what it does because speakers of a language all agree on its meaning, though the sound or printed form of the word bears no other relation, iconic or indexical, to that meaning. In English we call a dog a *dog*, in French they call it a *chien*. There's nothing about either sound (or written form) that makes it more or less suited to expressing that meaning.

This property of words was called the "arbitrariness of the sign" by another famous semiotician, Ferdinand de Saussure, who is widely regarded as the founder of the modern field of linguistics. Because of his enormous influence on the field, linguists have tended to take the arbitrariness of words for granted, and therefore to focus on symbolic representation. Indexical meaning in language has received much less attention (and that from anthropologists more than linguists); and iconic meaning, very little attention at all.

Some eastern European linguists, however, took Peirce's ideas and ran with them, applying them to language itself. One was Roman Jakobson, a Russian linguist who bounced around Europe and then immigrated to the United States at the start of World War II. One thing Jakobson sought to understand about language was the variety of functions played by linguistic forms, apart from their symbolic function. To describe these different functions, he appealed to the basic structure of communication, which he analyzed into six parts: sender, message, receiver, context, channel, and code. The first three are self-explanatory. Context is the physical and social situation in which a message is communicated. If two friends are sitting in a café chatting, the context consists of the other tables and customers nearby, other properties of the room where they're sitting, and the relationship that exists between the friends and their knowledge about each other's lives. *Channel* is the mode or medium of communication: writing, speaking face-to-face, speaking on the phone, and so on. *Code* is the set of conventions, or "rules," of the language being used.

In Jakobson's view, a verbal message can be characterized by the element of the communicative situation it highlights. It might focus on the context by singling out a nearby object and saying something about it. It might focus on the speaker by expressing his or her emotional state. It might focus on the receiver of the message by eliciting an emotional response. Each of these ways a message can relate to context Jakobson referred to as a "function." One of the most interesting functions is the poetic function, in which a message highlights its own form. The poetic function will be important when we come to the next section of the book, which focuses on sound. The chapters in this section examine the ways that meaning, in its various facets, can be used creatively in micromessages.

RELEVANCE

Networks of associations allow people to get from point A to point B when they go through the unconscious mental steps involved in interpreting a message. But the route is usually not direct. Some philosophers of language have thought about how people communicate indirectly and have concluded that we're quite good at it. Paul Grice is one of them. He showed that normal conversation follows certain underlying principles, which he called "maxims" and expressed in imperative form (as I've done with my chapter names). Don't be fooled by that presentation, though. Grice is not implying that people need lessons on how to talk to one another. He's saying that people naturally do these things when they're engaging in cooperative conversation. These maxims *describe* conversational behavior.

One maxim is "be relevant." From the perspective of someone being spoken to, it says that we always interpret a conversational partner's behavior as being relevant in some way to the ongoing interaction. When we do that, we make inferences that help us identify the meanings people intend to communicate to us. Social and cognitive scientist Dan Sperber and linguist Deirdre Wilson developed a theory, called relevance theory, that treats this maxim as the foundation of all human communication. We have evolved to communicate, and the human mind is a relevance machine. It takes in new information and recognizes how it relates to the situation at hand and the things we know and believe. Let's call that the *relevance principle.*

Recognizing relevance means recognizing someone's intention to communicate. Here's a simple example similar to one that Sperber and Wilson discuss in their book *Relevance.* Suppose you're sitting on a park bench chatting with a friend, and your friend suddenly but discreetly leans back, glancing at you to see if you notice her doing it. You recognize that she wants you to notice what she's doing. Your mind quickly casts about, thinking about why she would want you to notice. You realize that she's leaning back so you can see something. You look past her and observe a despised colleague—one you had just been talking about—sitting in the bench next to yours.

In this simple scenario, communication happened because you recognized an intention and you tried to understand how your friend's behavior could possibly be relevant to your conversation. In this case the communication was nonverbal, and that's an important part of Sperber and Wilson's point. All meanings, including the ones we communicate verbally, involve such a process of recognizing an intention. Meanings aren't determined solely by the conventional definitions of the words we use.

Grice used the idea of relevance to make sense of how people communicate indirectly using words. Some cases he discussed were fairly simple, such as the way we might say, "It's a little cold in here," when we want someone to close the window. Basically, a person who hears this statement thinks, "What am I supposed to *do* with this information?" In the search for relevance, that question is always paramount. The relevance principle is important for understanding micromessages because the less meaning that's explicitly encoded in a verbal message, the more that must be discovered in the search for relevance.

I

BE CLEAR

Although there is no substitute for merit in writing, clarity comes closest to being one.
—Strunk and White, *The Elements of Style*

We don't always have to be clever, thank goodness. Often simply being clear is enough.

When we talk about clarity in writing, we use a metaphor in which understanding a verbal message is like looking through something transparent to see the truth behind it. This metaphor treats meaning as if it were tangible and visible, and words as something we use to see meaning and show it to others. The words shouldn't get in the way; they're valuable to the extent that we don't notice them.

This view of language is common. It might even be considered the default way to think about language. It's reinforced by style guides like Strunk & White because they're typically written for newspaper reporters, student essay-writers, and others whose writing needs to be more informative than artistic or entertaining. Strunk and White never said that clarity was the be-all and end-all of writing, but in the quote that opens this chapter, they came close. Even in the realm of fiction writing, the influence of writers like Hemingway has placed a high premium on direct, succinct language.

I am not here to praise clarity or to bury it. Much of the rest of this book considers different ways to be clear, as well as aspects of style that go beyond being clear. Let's just recognize clarity as an important aim, and one suited especially well to certain modes of writing: headlines, informative tweets, email subject lines, and the like.

The world of product design has given us a slogan that captures the essence of this principle of microstyle while also following it: KEEP IT SIMPLE AND STUPID (or, sometimes, KEEP IT SIMPLE, STUPID), known as the *KISS principle*. Newspaper headlines often follow the KISS principle, especially when they're reporting hard news (as opposed to sports, cultural, and human interest stories). Even with less serious stories, the facts are sometimes so compelling that they need no embellishment.

Consider the following headlines, collected by journalist Larry D. Larsen for Poynter Online in the feature "1,000 Headlines in 460 Days":

MONKEY VISITS GERMAN PIZZERIA,
VANDALIZES TOILET

MAN WEARING CHICKEN SUIT ROBS KROGER

OHIO TEENS FORCED TO WALK THROUGH TOWN
WITH DONKEY

WOMAN CHASED BY FAKE ALIEN SUES
REALITY TV SHOW

The story about the monkey is as funny as the headline. The end of the first paragraph reports that the vandalism took place "even though the owner had tried to pacify the animal with salad and rolls." If it works for unhappy customers, why not try it with an unruly monkey? Headlines like these just can't be gussied up. Any attempt at cleverness here would be gilding the lily.

The simple, direct approach often serves local business owners quite nicely. Need new heels for your dress shoes? Talk to Angel at Angel's Shoe Repair. Need meat? Try Bob the Butcher. Sometimes just informing, as directly as possible, is all you need to do to grab the attention of your audience. Perhaps the purest form of this is advertising by specs and price—the kind of advertising electronics retailers do in the newspaper. It's a just-the-facts-ma'am approach. Bigger companies used to do this with their names: International Business Machines, American Broadcasting Corporation, etc. The strategy works when the product is something new or in high demand. When Microsoft started out, for example, microcomputer software for consumers was a novelty.

While simplicity has its practical side, it can also be a form of cleverness—a clean, acidic spritz of clarity on the oily smudges of confusion. In his book *In Defense of Food*, Michael Pollan sums up his advice about healthy eating with a simple maxim: "Eat food. Not too much. Mostly plants." The simplicity of this formulation is powerful and memorable because it contrasts so starkly with the complicated, counterintuitive, and often contradictory advice we've received over the years from nutrition experts:

- Eat mostly carbs.
- Avoid carbs and focus on protein.
- Eat margarine instead of butter.
- Margarine is worse than butter.

- Chocolate, alcohol, and coffee are bad for you.
- Chocolate, alcohol, and coffee might actually be good for you.

Sometimes simple clarity is the most surprising, and surprisingly effective, tool you can use in a message.

Ad slogans often opt for a crystal clear expression of what marketers like to call the "value proposition"—the description of what consumers have to gain from using a product. Here are some examples of admirable pith:

LISTERINE FIGHTS BAD BREATH

MILTON BRADLEY MAKES THE BEST GAMES
IN THE WORLD

GLASSES IN LESS THAN AN HOUR *(LensCrafters)*

I JUST SAVED A BUNCH OF MONEY
ON MY CAR INSURANCE *(Geico)*

TASTES GREAT, LESS FILLING *(Miller beer)*

The direct approach to slogans has been with us for a long time. Coca-Cola was using it just after the First World War:

THERE'S A DELICIOUS FRESHNESS TO THE TASTE OF
COCA-COLA *(1917)*

IT SATISFIES THIRST *(1919)*

Sometimes advertisers make a game of being clear and thorough rather than clear and succinct, as in this NyQuil slogan:

THE NIGHT-TIME, SNIFFLING, SNEEZING,

COUGHING, ACHING, STUFFY HEAD, FEVER,

SO-YOU-CAN-REST MEDICINE

or in the McDonald's Big Mac jingle:

TWO ALL-BEEF PATTIES, SPECIAL SAUCE, LETTUCE,

CHEESE, PICKLES, ONIONS, ON A SESAME SEED BUN

Despite their length, these phrases show great economy of expression. The first memorably lists all the symptoms that NyQuil treats, and the second lists all the ingredients of a Big Mac.

It can be a challenge to be clear even when you're talking about real things. What if you only have a few words to communicate about something that doesn't exist yet? That's the challenge of the pitch. If you want to make a movie or start a company and you're looking for funding, you need a pitch. In fact, you need several versions of your pitch, all of different lengths, to fit different pitching opportunities. You've probably heard of the "elevator pitch"— a statement of a business idea that's brief enough to be delivered during an elevator ride. Even that's not short enough for some purposes, though.

Now, some entrepreneurs are encouraged to develop an "escalator pitch." A pitch that lasts as long as an escalator ride, right? No. A pitch short enough to make when you're on the up escalator and your funding prospect is on the down escalator, passing by. This idea caught on when Stowe Boyd solicited "twitpitches" to determine which companies he would meet with at the 2008 Web 2.0 Expo in San Francisco. A twitpitch is submitted via Twitter and therefore must be no longer than 140 characters, the maximum length of a Twitter message, or *tweet*.

If you think an escalator pitch sounds challenging, consider what some investment-seeking entrepreneurs reach for: a *high-*

concept pitch. This is a microgenre taken from Hollywood. A Hollywood high-concept pitch is an extremely short phrase that encapsulates a movie, often by comparing it to another movie. The classic sci-fi thriller *Alien*, for example, has been described as "*Jaws* in space." The title of the movie *Snakes on a Plane* is itself a high-concept pitch.

Jane Espenson, who has written for television shows such as *Buffy the Vampire Slayer*, reveals an interesting fact: Though TV writers don't use high-concept pitches for episodes—they're expected to present worked-out story ideas—the concepts that actually get picked up and turned into episodes are often not the fully worked-out ones. Instead, they're the ones based on single sentences thrown out at the end of a longer pitch. Jane sold two ideas to *Star Trek: The Next Generation* using single sentences. One was "Data is stranded on a Luddite planet," and the other was "Every time we go warp speed we're actually destroying the fabric of the universe." Jane speculates that the one-sentence pitches are bought because the writers who hear them are able to flesh them out in their own minds. They want to be able to fill in the details. In this case, there was a benefit to leaving *out* information. Clarity means finding the right level of detail for the circumstances.

Certain contexts, such as the pitch context, call for maximum clarity and succinctness. But that's not true of all contexts.

WHEN IS IT OK TO BE UNCLEAR?

This is a tricky question. As Strunk and White say, "Be obscure clearly!" That is, clarity of a sort is always a goal, even when it seems not to be. But that complicates the issue. Let's start with a very commonsense idea of clear message, and consider when it is and isn't important for a message to conform to that model.

It's OK for your message to be indirect, unexpected, ambiguous, or even a little vague, but it shouldn't leave people scratching their heads. They should at least know where to start looking for relevance. If you can't make sense of a company's slogan, you certainly won't understand its mission. Camera maker Olympus uses the slogan YOUR VISION, OUR FUTURE. When noun phrases are used like this, without any other context, the receiver of a message should be able to figure out what they refer to. In this case it's difficult. The word *vision* is clearly employed for its double meaning. Literally it refers to customers' visual perception, so it relates to photography. Figuratively it must refer to the way customers see the future. But why does Olympus say "our future"? Does that mean belonging to Olympus, or to people in general? If the latter, why the contrast with "your vision"? It's hard to make sense of this.

Twitter redesigned its home page in the spring of 2010. It got rid of the old description of the service, which focused on the idea of making "updates," and tried to capture the wide range of ways people now use the service. Because Twitter is new and unique, it should describe itself well on its home page. This is what appeared there before the change:

SHARE AND DISCOVER WHAT'S HAPPENING RIGHT NOW,
ANYWHERE IN THE WORLD.

Here's how the new description began:

TWITTER IS A RICH SOURCE OF INSTANT
INFORMATION. STAY UPDATED. KEEP OTHERS
UPDATED. IT'S A WHOLE THING.

Frederic Lardinois of ReadWriteWeb said this new explanation of Twitter "sounds a little odd," and I'd have to agree. The sentence "It's a whole thing" might sound colloquial and friendly, but it's completely uninformative. As Steve Spillman wrote in *Slate* magazine:

> *Seriously, Twitter, "It's a whole thing"? That's the way I describe Twitter, but I'm a 20-something New York hipster, or something close to it. And I'm usually not trying to get millions of people to sign up, or whatever you are trying to do with this. This doesn't say anything about how Twitter works.*

Sometimes slogans involve puzzling presuppositions. ConAgra Foods introduced the slogan THE RIGHT KIND OF FOOD COMPANY. There's an implicit contrast here with the "wrong" kind of food company. But what kind of company is that? And why would ConAgra want to call such a company to mind? This slogan hints at a world of nefarious motives in the food industry that people probably wouldn't even think of on their own. Some slogans confound with bizarre grammar. RCAT Systems, which manufactures wireless data devices for aircraft, used the slogan YOU PUSH THE LIMITS. WE MEASURE IT. It's not clear what the antecedent of the singular pronoun *it* is supposed to be, since the word *limits* is plural.

Sometimes a message is unclear not because it fails to present information clearly but because it buries the information under irrelevant elaborations. Consider the following tagline for the movie *SpaceCamp*:

> THEY CAME TO SPACECAMP WITH THE DREAM OF BECOMING ASTRONAUTS. SUDDENLY . . . WITHOUT WARNING . . . BEFORE THEY WERE READY . . . THEY WERE LAUNCHED INTO SPACE.

The *Huffington Post* calls this one of the worst taglines of all time. When I read this I fell asleep before I got to the punch line, which is "Kids in space!" In the newspaper world this mistake is called "burying the lead."

Let's consider a case in more detail. There was a lot of anticipation among technophiles about mobile phones that would use Google's Android open mobile platform. When the Verizon/ Google partnership came out with a line of Android phones, called Droid, it advertised them with the following slogan:

A BARE-KNUCKLED BUCKET OF DOES

The word *does* is intended as a verb—the third-person singular form of the verb *do*—turned into a noun. The slogan is meant to highlight the phone's impressive specifications and capabilities —what it can *do*. But the use of *does* is grammatically bizarre. Though verbs are often turned into nouns in English, people usually use the bare form of the verb, which would be *do* in this case. The straightforward grammatical interpretation of this slogan, though one that is contextually nonsensical, would treat *does* as the plural of the noun *doe*, meaning 'female deer.' People quickly figure out that this isn't the intended meaning, but not without first wondering what those deer are doing in that bucket.

Another confusing thing about this slogan is the mixed metaphor. The phone is not actually a bucket, of course, so that's one metaphor. And the phone is not literally bare-knuckled, so that's another. The expression *bare-knuckled* is an allusion to a fighting context: when the gloves come off, things get serious. *Bare-knuckled* modifies *bucket*, and you sort of want that modification to make some sense in metaphor world. But what does it mean for a bucket to be bare-knuckled?

The Droid slogan at least gets high marks for alliteration and assonance. The emphasized vowels in *knuckled, bucket,* and *does* are identical, and the "k" sound is repeated after that vowel in *knuckled* and *bucket*.

Lack of clarity is an aesthetic offense as well as a communicative one. It may be true that no one really believes the slogan A BARE-KNUCKLED BUCKET OF DOES refers to female deer, but that interpretation is just hanging around, distractingly, like an annoying coworker. The incorrect reading affects the way the slogan *feels*. Any negative or irrelevant interpretation that seems unintentional reflects badly on the person who created the message, and that detracts from the message itself.

The importance of clarity depends on the purpose of a message. Hard news headlines and informative tweets are for communicating accurately with few words. For those micromessages, clarity is usually essential. But sometimes headlines present confusing messages to pique interest in a story. Here's a headline that appeared on the ABC News website on January 21, 2010:

NO MORE JESUS RIFLES

The story was about a company that agreed to stop putting Bible verses on the gun sights it supplied to the American military. There's no way you'd get that from the headline, which was created just to grab people and make them wonder, "What in the Lord's name is a Jesus rifle?" It worked on me.

Clarity becomes less important when messages serve the mysterious aims of what we call *branding*. Names and slogans are often not intended to be informative. Rather, they're supposed to evoke ideas and feelings. To achieve this, they often communicate indirectly. A name *can* be informative but need not be. It has two real purposes. One is simply to symbolically represent something— a company, a product, what have you. As Saussure would point out, any arbitrary but pronounceable string of sounds can do that. The main function of a brand name, however, is to add conceptual and emotional depth to people's ideas about a product, company, or service. This can work very indirectly indeed. Does the name

Apple communicate clearly about personal computing devices? Well, given a very straightforward understanding of clarity, not at all. And that's a good thing. Apple conjures all kinds of associations, some literary and cultural, some based on direct experience. A brand name need not communicate unambiguously. In fact, multiple meanings and fuzzy ideas are highly desirable, as long as they're appropriate.

The name Apple, as indirect as it is, immediately makes a certain kind of sense. The enterprise software company Knouen, on the other hand, has a name that's as difficult to make sense of as it is to pronounce. LibraryThing, a social network for book lovers, just gives up trying to communicate after the *library* part.

Some names are meant to be enigmatic, which isn't the same as being unclear. Or rather, it's being unclear in a forgivable way. The company name 37signals, for example, is a mystery to most people. Those who happen to look around on the company website find that the name refers to the number of unexplained, potentially intelligent signals from outer space. This kind of name isn't trying to be clear—the questions it raises are part of the point. For names to get away with this strategy, they have to reward curiosity by being very interesting, like 37signals does. And it doesn't hurt to have poetic properties, like the appealing alliteration in 37signals (see Chapter 12).

Clarity serves different purposes, and even a lack of clarity, done in the right way, can add expressive power to a micromessage.

2

CHOOSE THE RIGHT WORD

W hen you construct a message, words are your building
materials. Start with weak materials and your message
won't hold up, no matter how it's put together.

You might consider the dictionary the final word on words.
But "the" dictionary doesn't exist. There are many dictionaries,
ranging from the *Oxford English Dictionary* (the paragon of lexi-
cography) to the humblest online slang dictionary. A good dictionary represents a remarkable intellectual achievement, but all
dictionaries are imperfect, and most are created under enormous
constraints of time and resources. Not to mention that their stated
goal borders on the impossible: capturing in a permanent form a
dynamic and elusive phenomenon.

Language isn't something that can be captured, in a book
or anywhere else. Language is a fluid interplay of human activity and cognition. Dictionaries are fascinating, delightful, and
extremely useful for certain purposes, but they don't capture any
of the power of words that people feel every day. Words evoke

ideas and moods in a way that's difficult to understand or explain.

Though words aren't butterflies, the perfect one is an elusive beast, and there's an art to finding it. The French expression *le mot juste* describes the exact word or phrase needed to convey the right meaning. If finding the right word in French is difficult, it's even tougher in English, which has a bigger vocabulary. Or at least, it's more like finding a needle in a haystack. French has borrowed few words from other languages, in part because of the French Academy's efforts to maintain the integrity of the language. English, on the other hand, has welcomed borrowed words, snowballing through the world, getting bigger and bigger. The *Oxford English Dictionary* has more than 300,000 entries.

Of course, some English words are basically synonyms. We have, for example, the Old English–derived word *kiss*, and we also have the Latin-derived word *osculate*, a fancy way to say the same thing. But some linguists believe that true synonyms are rare. Where people see different words, they expect different meanings, so they tend to find subtle shades of meaning to differentiate what seem like synonyms. The difference in meaning might be more a matter of how the words feel than what they refer to. In English, for example, original Old English words like *kiss* sound familiar and intimate, while Latin-based words like *osculate* sound detached and clinical.

The tendency to distinguish synonyms is also shown by toddlers learning to speak. Eve Clark, professor of linguistics at Stanford University, turned that observation into a "no synonymy" principle to explain how children learn so many words so fast. She and others argue that children would have an easier time identifying all the meanings expressed by words if they were to assume that different words express different things about the world. There's a certain commonsense logic to this idea. Imagine you point to a yellow balloon and say to a child, "Balloon. Yellow. The balloon is yellow." Without a no-synonymy assumption, a child might believe that *balloon* and *yellow* both basically mean 'balloon.' But, if they take the different sound of *yellow* as a cue for a different meaning, they're more likely to assume it refers to the color (or shape or size or something else the child notices). So a bias against synonymy may be an adaptive mechanism that helps explain children's remarkably rapid vocabulary development, and it may linger on in adulthood and affect the way words are used and change in meaning over time.

The tendency to distinguish words in adulthood is the relevance principle at work. When we're interacting with people, we try to relate their behavior to what's going on. We try to determine what makes it relevant to the interaction, as we saw in the park bench example. One aspect of behavior is word choice. If you use one word rather than another in a given context, people assume there's a reason, and that reason would be understood as a subtle difference in meaning. As E. B. White put it in Strunk and White's *Elements of Style*: "Never call a stomach a tummy without good reason." Fine meaning distinctions and shades of meaning come naturally to us, because the relevance principle encourages us to search for them.

How, then, do you pick a word? First you need to get the basic meaning right. Otherwise you might end up, like Reebok, calling a women's athletic shoe Incubus. An incubus is a demon from medieval folklore that rapes women in their sleep. Its female counterpart is a succubus. So if you aren't absolutely certain what a word means, at least look it up in the dictionary.

Word choice goes way beyond mere definitions, though. For starters, a word may have a technical definition that differs markedly in emphasis from its popular use. Consider the electric motorcycle called Enertia, clearly based on the word *inertia*. The technical meaning of *inertia* is something like "the tendency of an object to maintain direction and velocity unless acted upon by an external force." That might seem pretty appropriate for a motorcycle. But the word *inertia* is typically used for a very special subcase covered by the technical meaning: the case in which the velocity of an object is zero. When people talk about inertia, they usually mean the tendency of an object to remain at rest—which is compatible with the technical definition. The implications for naming are vast, though. No one wants a motorcycle that has a tendency to remain at rest. The real kicker is that this is an electric motorcycle, which is likely to be met with some skepticism among cycling aficionados and be perceived as less powerful than an internal-combustion motorcycle.

Understanding a word's circumstances of use—the topic of the conversation or other discourse in which it's embedded, the social or institutional setting in which it's used, the general activity it refers to, etc.—helps determine a word's meaning in any particular instance of its use. When a word is habitually used in the same context, we can commit our collective understanding of this context to our memories and make it a part of the word meaning that we carry around in our heads. It becomes a portable context. If we encounter a word out of context, we can project this default context onto it.

This is a key to the way words work, and it helps to explain why they don't just express meanings like the ones you read about in dictionary definitions. For its definition to make any sense, a word has to activate rich networks of background knowledge, beliefs, and assumptions. Charles Fillmore, professor emeritus of linguistics at UC Berkeley, calls these knowledge networks *frames*. They're at work all the time in our normal vocabulary and can create subtle differences between words—even words that seem like synonyms.

The nouns *ground* and *land*, for example, both refer to the dry part of the Earth's surface and are listed as synonyms in *Roget's Thesaurus*. But they're used in different contexts. We say "on the ground" in contrast to "in the air," and "on land" in contrast to "in the water" or "at sea." The word *ground* evokes a frame related to standing, climbing, jumping, and flying; the word *land* evokes a frame related to swimming and boating. That's something we speakers of English understand implicitly, even if we don't notice it or think much about it.

The difference between *ground* and *land* isn't a matter of literal meaning, the way some people understand what that is. In the tradition of formal semantics, which attempts to analyze linguistic meaning using the tools of formal logic, meaning is a matter of truth conditions, the circumstances under which factual statements are true and false. In that tradition, which is favored by many American linguistics departments, if you want to know whether *ground* and *land* have different meanings, you ask something like this: "Can you imagine a situation in which the statement 'I am lying on the ground' is true and the statement 'I am lying on (the) land' is false?" If the answer is no, then the words don't have different meanings. If your impulse is to say, "No, but you'd only say that second sentence if you'd been swimming or on a boat," then you're appealing to frames to distinguish the words.

Ultimately the difference between *ground* and *land* isn't something that formal semanticists are interested in (which is one reason why people who use words creatively don't tend to be very interested in formal semantics). It's a matter of the networks of background knowledge and assumptions associated with these words. Frames exert a pressure on people to use words in certain ways, but they don't require it. Consider the number of Google results that I got for searches on the following four phrases:

Search Phrase	Number of Results
"dry land"	2,390,000
"solid ground"	1,910,000
"dry ground"	425,000
"solid land"	68,800

People talk a lot about "dry land" and "solid ground," much less about "dry ground," and much less still about "solid land." In the first two phrases, the adjectives evoke the contrasts that the nouns make us expect. In the third and fourth phrases, the adjectives focus on unexpected contrasts.

Frames can also imply different judgments about the same phenomenon. The words *thrifty* and *stingy* both describe people who don't spend much money, but *thrifty* treats that quality as a virtue, while *stingy* treats it as a flaw.

George Lakoff has written about framing in political discourse. Framing involves using the frames associated with words to influence the way people think about issues. To use one of Lakoff's favorite examples, fiscal conservatives engage in clever framing when they talk about "tax relief" as opposed to "tax cuts." The word *cuts* sounds destructive and negative. The word *relief*, on the other hand, implies that taxes are some kind of burden or malady, and that reducing taxes returns people to a normal healthy state. That's framing at work.

Every word choice offers an opportunity for framing. In a message of just one word or a few words, it can make all the difference. Consider the story of Lilipip, a young company that started out creating children's educational videos for mobile devices. Its tagline was "Feeding curiosity daily." I spoke to Ksenia Oustiougova, founder and CEO of Lilipip, about the tagline and how she came up with it. Oustiougova, who takes pride in her frank manner, saw Lilipip as the solution to a problem: too many stupid people. Her dream was to turn mobile phones and similar devices into educational tools for kids. Though the company was about education, she told me she avoided that word in her tagline, her other marketing materials, and her investment pitches. This is a great example of smart framing and word choice.

The words *education* and *curiosity* both relate to Lilipip's mission. But *education* places the concept of learning in an institutional context and presents it from the perspective of someone doing the teaching. It calls to mind school, homework, compulsory lessons, and things that are supposed to be good for you. Not to mention educational policy, school board meetings, and neverending disputes about the curriculum. The word *curiosity*, on the other hand, presents learning from the perspective of the person doing it. It names the inner drive that makes learning intrinsically satisfying. It calls to mind a scientist working late into the night, a reporter breaking a big story, or a detective tracking down a killer. It also evokes Curious George and "Curiosity killed the cat." *Curiosity* sounds interesting, fun, exciting, and even dangerous. *Education* sounds, well, a little boring.

The words *curiosity* and *education* occupy different terrain in our mental landscape. Oustiougova recognized that and chose well. Associating the Lilipip videos with *curiosity* rather than *education* made them something people wanted to watch, not something they felt they should watch.

The tagline's use of the word *feeding* also achieves clever framing with metaphor, one of the most powerful tools of microstyle (see Chapter 7). *Feeding* sets up a metaphorical correspondence between education and nourishment. Note that Oustiougova didn't make up this metaphor—it's pervasive in English (and other languages). We talk, for example, about "food for thought" and "digesting" ideas. This metaphor also ties in with other relevant metaphors that are entrenched in our language and culture. We have the notion of "personal growth," which treats intellectual and emotional improvement as if it were physical enlargement. Treating things that foster long-term development and well-being, like education, as nourishment extends this metaphor in a natural way. Yet the immediate act of eating is pleasurable. *Feeding* conveys the personal enjoyment that comes from satisfying curiosity, and it also does some of the work that the more earnest word *education* would have done.

The phrase "feeding curiosity" is also ambiguous, but in a good way (see Chapter 8). Because curiosity can be understood metaphorically as hunger, feeding curiosity means satisfying it. But feeding something can also mean sustaining it, literally and metaphorically. If you feed a rumor, you help it survive and spread. So, too, with feeding curiosity. When you learn, you experience the satisfaction of one hunger and a new hunger for more learning. Oustiougova found the perfect words to capture that in her tagline.

When I help a client solve a naming or verbal branding problem, sometimes the best solution consists of just one word. Needless to say, word choice is critical in that case.

Sometimes an entity or phenomenon is so laden with significance that the mere mention of it makes for a powerful message. In a famous line from the movie *The Graduate*, a middle-aged man gives "the graduate," played by Dustin Hoffman, a bit of career advice: "I have one word for you: *plastics*." For the character who spoke the line, that one word represented the future and unlimited opportunity, though Hoffman's expression makes it clear that it didn't have the same resonance for the protagonist. The one word is not always so mundane, and it's not always used in such a literal way. Movie titles often get by with one word. Here are some classics:

> ALIEN
> DELIVERANCE
> JAWS
> PSYCHO
> REDS
> TRAFFIC
> TRUST
> UNFORGIVEN
> VERTIGO

Sometimes the subject matter of a movie is so compelling that a mere mention of it makes a good title; consider *Alien*, *Psycho*, and *Reds*. Sometimes, however, the real interest of a movie is more abstract, and a word that relates obliquely to the story is more effective. Alfred Hitchcock's movie *Vertigo*, for example, was about a murder, a love affair, memory and loss, and a police detective with a work-related injury. The title, however, perfectly captures the queasy, off-balance feeling the film induces in the viewer, as well as the psychological state of the protagonist.

Naming, as previously mentioned, is a special exercise in relevance creation. When you encounter a name for a new company or product, even if the name seems "arbitrary," your mind subconsciously finds the network of ideas that connects the name to the company or product. That network is one of the most important aspects of a brand.

Our natural tendency to hunt for relevance helps explain why the most descriptive names are not the best names. One of the least successful ways to name a company, product, or service is to choose the word or phrase that most clearly describes it. That distinguishes names from the direct slogans we saw in the previous chapter. For most good names, the network of meaning is indirect. There are both legal and strategic reasons for this. Legally, a name can't be trademarked if it's too descriptive of the product or service it represents. You can't trademark a name like "Delicious Foods" or "Big Strong Trash Bags." But even if you could, you probably wouldn't want to, because names like that add little to a brand. They're too one-dimensional.

If the search for relevance is a journey, then baldly descriptive names are like a trip to the grocery store: they're short, and you don't see anything very interesting along the way. Suggestive names, on the other hand, lead you through exciting mental territory that makes for a memorable trip.

Let's take a look at a name that works. In 1976, a young businessman had to think of a name for his new company, which sold computer circuit boards that were hand-built by his friend. They were made for electronics enthusiasts who could hook them up to keyboards and video displays to make rudimentary computers. To reflect his focus on the individual hobbyist, the entrepreneur wanted to choose a friendly name. Drawing on his experience working in the orchards of Oregon, the businessman decided to call the company Apple Computer.

Apples don't have much to do with computers; I mentioned Apple earlier as a name that succeeds by communicating indirectly. But the frames that are called to mind by the word *apple* create associations that make Apple Computer a great name. This name is a model solution to a problem faced by all technology companies: how to make something that's fundamentally abstract and mysterious seem tangible and appealing. Apple, you may recall, is largely responsible for turning computers into popular consumer commodities. Steve Jobs's choice of company name managed to make computers seem fun, approachable, and desirable. Of course, it wasn't just the name that achieved that. It was the user interface and the design and the packaging and the marketing. But the name Apple set the tone. How?

First, there's the obvious cultural symbolism of apples. They're associated with school (an apple for the teacher) and therefore with childhood and learning. They call to mind the story of Isaac Newton having his epiphany about gravity when an apple fell on his head. In the story of Adam and Eve, the apple represents knowledge and sex. Who doesn't want those things? The apple also represents sin, and that contributes to the hip, rebellious image that Apple projected with its 1984 TV ad for the Macintosh. The ad featured a lone iconoclast disrupting some kind of Orwellian mass brainwashing event by smashing a giant video screen with a single hammer throw. The apple, unlike that heavy-handed image, is the perfect symbol for the subversive power that was promised by the personal computer. The Apple logo, with the little bite taken out of it, is an obvious reference to the idea of eating from the tree of knowledge.

This kind of quasi-literary symbolism forms only part of the story, though. The deeper power of the name Apple comes from our everyday experiences with actual apples. They are, in a sense, the perfect consumer commodity: they're ubiquitous and inexpensive, you grasp them in your hand and literally consume them, and they're delicious. For almost everyone, they're old childhood friends: cut into little pieces and cooked into sauce for babies, put into school lunch boxes and toted around, and baked into pies. It's these deeply rooted sensory memories of apples that make Apple a great name. Nothing is more familiar, more accessible, or less intimidating than an apple.

Steve Jobs probably didn't think of all these things when he named his company. He probably just thought that the name Apple "fit." Good names usually work subconsciously. And they can be effective even if people don't recognize their "real" rationale. Marc Hershon, who worked as a namer at Lexicon Branding, created the name BlackBerry for the now ubiquitous mobile email device made by Research In Motion. During the first creative session, he looked at the little prototype device the client had brought in, which was black and covered with tiny keys, and said, "It looks like an electronic blackberry." The client, who was from Canada, had never heard the word *blackberry* before—to him they're *loganberries*. He was delighted by the fanciful idea of a berry that's black, and the name survived through several rounds of creative work to emerge as the winner.

For every hit, however, there's a miss. The wrong word choice can really make a name or other message fall flat. Take the online music service called Fairtilizer. Its name is based on the word *fertilizer* and contains the word *fair* as well. Now, lurking somewhere behind the word *fertilizer* is the basis for a very appealing metaphor: something that encourages growth. But we all know that *fertilizer* is manure (or chemicals). People sometimes use the word *fertilizer* when they're too polite to say *bullshit*. The word *fair* isn't any better. It can imply evenhandedness. But it also means so-so. Not great, not good—just fair. So these word choices don't work in English-speaking countries the way they were probably expected to (Fairtilizer is a Swiss company).

Bad word choice is often the result of poor translation and cross-cultural misunderstanding. No one in the United States would choose to call a manufacturer of children's toys Bullyland, but someone in Germany did.

Some odd word choices work in spite of themselves. Consider Yelp, the name of a website where people post reviews of restaurants and other local businesses. Yelping is a shrill sound that a dog makes, usually when it's in distress—not a nice way to characterize the reviews on the site. Nevertheless, my own personal and very unscientific survey suggests that people like the name (as well as the site). Perhaps people respond to the idea of feeling pain and letting the world know about it.

Sometimes people make questionable word choices because they're straining to be poetic or clever. The rhyme of the name SmugMug, for an online photo site, comes at a cost: the word *smug* describes a human quality that inspires resentment and hostility in people.

Sometimes a word with an appropriate meaning is poorly chosen because it resembles another word with a less appropriate one. Bazaarvoice provides Amazon-like product reviews for online retailers. The word *bazaar* seems appropriate because it means 'marketplace.' Unfortunately, it also sounds like *bizarre*, and no retailer wants its product reviews written in a bizarre voice.

When looking for the right word, pay careful attention to the type of situation that that word conjures up in your mind, and the kinds of inferences it points you toward. When connecting these dots becomes second nature, you'll be a veritable bloodhound when it comes to finding *le mot juste*.

3

PAINT A PICTURE

Sensory information makes messages attention-getting, absorbing, and memorable. Evolution has shaped our brains to help us perceive, move around in, and manipulate the physical world. We're best at thinking with the information provided by our bodies—visual images, sounds, smells, tastes, tactile sensations, and body awareness. We can recall sensory images instantaneously, and we find abstract ideas easier to remember if we associate them with sensory images. Concepts that we can associate with sensory impressions, and visual images in particular, come naturally to us.

In the 1970s, Eleanor Rosch, a psychologist at Berkeley, did some foundational research on human categorization. Categories form hierarchies, ranging from the extremely general (for example, "thing") to the extremely specific (for example, "the scratched wooden chair I'm sitting on right now"). Categories somewhere in the middle of this hierarchy, not too general and not too specific, have a number of properties that make them special—they're the categories that are most likely to be expressed by words in any language, and for which children tend to first learn words. One special property of these "basic-level categories" is that they're the most general categories for which we can form mental images. Most of us can conjure up an image of a generic pear, but not of a generic piece of fruit. That makes "pear" a basic-level category.

The properties of basic-level categories suggest that concepts associated with mental images have a privileged status for people. Writers, of course, use images all the time to make their stories come to life. Here's a six-word memoir from the *Smith Magazine* website:

> *Window box, Modest lawn, Wildflower meadow.*
> —*Andrew_Hardy, February 5, 2008*

In this little story, the course of a life is depicted in three vivid images. When we picture each one, we inevitably imagine the situation in which it's embedded. A window box is for a tiny garden in an apartment. A lawn surrounds a house in the suburbs. Meadows are in the countryside. These three simple images instantly create a sense of movement (from city to country) and of growth (from small and modest to large and lush).

I always remind my naming clients that there's a practical advantage to using words that evoke a visual image: you can use the image as the basis for a logo, as well as other visual branding elements that might appear on a product package, website, or promotional brochure. Consider companies such as Apple, Pizza Hut, and Shell, whose logos depict an apple, a little roof, and a shell, respectively. Even if a company makes no explicit use of the visual images evoked by its name, those images can still be at work in the minds of customers and potential customers. The name Amazon, for example, might help us picture the flow of goods as a moving river, and the name Caterpillar might help us visualize the way the tracks of construction vehicles grip the ground.

Sensory appeals aren't always visual ones. Advertisers often call attention to the other sensuous qualities of products. A classic example is the M&M's candy slogan:

MELTS IN YOUR MOUTH, NOT IN YOUR HAND

created by the legendary adman Rosser Reeves (who also invented the short television ad spot while working on Eisenhower's 1952 presidential election campaign). The "melts in your mouth" part vividly evokes the feeling of eating chocolate. The melting in the hands part gives us a pressing reason to avoid competing products—fear of getting messy.

Names like Yahoo!, Yelp, and Twitter engage our auditory imaginations, as do slogans like SNAP! CRACKLE! POP! (for Rice Krispies) and the book and movie title *Bang the Drum Slowly*. Other movie titles, such as *Chocolat, Like Water for Chocolate, Wild Strawberries, Taste of Cherry*, and *A Taste of Honey*, make a gustatory impression. Still others, like *Body Heat, Silk Stockings, Blue Velvet*, and *Heat and Dust*, appeal to sensations on the skin.

Coca-Cola has tried hard over the years to link its product to the primal feeling of thirst:

THIRST REMINDS YOU—DRINK COCA-COLA *(1926)*

THIRST AND TASTE FOR COCA-COLA ARE
THE SAME THING *(1926)*

THE BEST FRIEND THIRST EVER HAD *(1939)*

THIRST STOPS HERE *(1939)*

Sensory images lend themselves to exaggeration and can lead to outlandishness. Beverage companies, for example, seem to try to out-awesome each other with their sensory associations. While A&W Root Beer made the modest claim that it would give us THAT FROSTY MUG SENSATION, Nestea upped the ante by inviting us to TAKE THE NESTEA PLUNGE, implying that a sip of instant iced tea is as refreshing as submerging your entire body in cold water. Ocean Spray promised a veritable tsunami of refreshment with CRAVE THE WAVE.

Besides being hyperbolic, some images can just be vivid in the wrong way. A tech startup that allowed people to highlight web pages called itself, for some inexplicable reason, BookGoo. The image evoked by this name, while vivid, isn't exactly pleasant. I think of something nasty that makes the pages of an old library book stick together. The sound symbolism of this name (see Chapter 13) strengthens that unfortunate association: the pronunciation gets "stuck" for a moment between the "k" and "g" sounds. Then there's the 1990s slogan from fast-food restaurant Carl's Jr. The restaurant ran a TV ad campaign featuring shots of people eating its burgers messily and ending with the slogan IF IT DOESN'T GET ALL OVER THE PLACE, IT DOESN'T BELONG IN YOUR FACE. The gross-out appeal of this message might work with a certain demographic, but for the rest of us it's off-putting in the extreme.

A sensation can be evoked with just a word or two, so sensory appeals are a common feature of microstyle. Visual images, in particular, are well suited to short messages. In fact, microstyle has a multifaceted kinship with graphic design. First, it's the verbal equivalent. If a novel is like a painting, and a scientific paper like a technical illustration, then a micromessage is like a bold graphic. It uses simple elements to maximum effect, can be noticed in a cluttered environment, and communicates in an instant.

Second, words and pictures just go together naturally. They're combined on posters, postcards, and product packages; in comics and captioned photos; and of course, in print ads. Both graphic design and microstyle reached their full potential in the print ad, where they typically appear together. The modern age of advertising began with the creative team, consisting of an art director (the picture person) and a copywriter (the word person) working together to realize a single creative idea, expressed partly in words and partly in pictures. The creative team was introduced in the 1960s by the legendary firm Doyle Dane Bernbach, which created famous ad campaigns for the Volkswagen Beetle, Avis Rent A Car System (WE TRY HARDER), and Life cereal (HEY, MIKEY!). The first creative team consisted of Bill Bernbach, the word guy, and Paul Rand, the designer who created the IBM logo and many other iconic brand images.

When an art director and a copywriter collaborate, they decide together which aspects of their message should be depicted visually and which should be evoked verbally. The visuals aren't there just to illustrate a fully fleshed-out text—they do more of the communicative heavy lifting. That allows the copy to be briefer and more elliptical.

A verbal landscape cluttered with print ads, television spots, and web ads has no doubt accustomed us to seeing verbal fragments —individual words, phrases, or sentences—as pointers to fuller meanings that have to be worked out from context. They've given us all a natural eye for microstyle.

This cultural pressure to bring our visual understanding to bear on verbal messages reinforces our naturally multimodal nature. There's a visual dimension to our most basic thought processes (even in the visually impaired), and visualization plays an important role in our understanding of words and our interpretation of verbal messages. Psychological studies have repeatedly shown that concepts evoked by words are easier to remember when they bring to mind clear visual images. Mnemonic devices for remembering people's names typically relate the names to memorable visual images. Albert Einstein even commented on the visual basis of his mathematical thinking. In a letter to psychologist Jacques Hadamard, Einstein wrote,

> *The physical entities which seem to serve as elements in thought are certain signs which can be "voluntarily" reproduced and combined . . . [They] are, in my case, of visual and some of muscular type.*

Though we like to think in images, we don't always think about things that we can see, hear, smell, feel, or taste. Metaphor enables us to use sensory images to talk—and think—about abstract and complex things in a simple, vivid, memorable way. The names Apple and BlackBerry metaphorically use the look and feel of fruits to add vividness to technological products—and to help us understand something about them. The familiar feeling of grasping an apple helps call attention to the fact that Apple's products are easy to use. The little keys on the BlackBerry from Research In Motion resemble the little segments of blackberries. The name Twitter uses the cheerful sound of birds as an instantly recognizable aural image for a new multivocal form of communication. The power of metaphor, as demonstrated by these examples, will be our focus in Chapter 7.

One of the keys of microstyle is the way verbal messages unlock nonverbal ways to understand things. Pictures and other sense impressions are important even when we communicate with a handful of words.

4

PUSH BUTTONS

Effective micromessages often push our emotional buttons. Making people feel things can be manipulation, art, or (more likely) something in between. At their worst, emotional appeals stir hatred and other negative emotions and take advantage of our weaknesses and insecurities. At their best, emotional appeals urge us to do good and to understand ourselves and others. Honest but less dramatic emotional appeals show us why something should matter to us. The integrity of an emotional appeal depends on whether the emotion evoked is constructive or destructive, whether it's real or illusory, and what action the appeal urges a person to take. Making people feel inadequate is cruel, as is promising them happiness that you can't deliver.

Emotions help us think. Antonio Damasio, professor of neuroscience and director of the Brain and Creativity Institute at the University of Southern California, believes that emotions assist with cognitive tasks like reasoning and decision making. When we reason about situations and predict different outcomes, we use our emotions to evaluate the hypothetical outcomes and to inform our decisions. Imagine you're giving a presentation tomorrow and need to prepare, but you also feel like popping in a DVD and relaxing. Opting to prepare is the responsible choice, but it's not merely a matter of reason winning out over emotion. Your choice still involves emotion: you imagine the scenario in which you watch the movie and find yourself, the next day, standing in front of a group of colleagues unprepared. The queasy feeling elicited by that embarrassing (but imaginary) situation nudges you toward the right path. Imagining consequences can make a bad decision painful and a good one pleasant. Of course, sometimes we choose to ignore this built-in warning system and make bad decisions anyway.

Emotions can add vividness to thoughts and the messages that express them. Like color and shape, they function as important elements of our experience that add detail to what we remember and imagine. I heard a radio interview in which a thorough city-planning expert was called "a belt-and-suspenders guy." Literally, a belt-and-suspenders guy would be a guy who *really* doesn't want his pants to fall down. This idiom gives us not only a vivid mental image, but an emotional hook as well: the potential for embarrassment. Of course, I have no attachment to that fellow on the radio, and I don't really care if his pants fall down. But then again, I do. Humans are rubberneckers and gossipers; we're almost as interested in others' emotions as in our own. And those other people don't even have to be real. When Maytag used the slogan OUR REPAIRMEN ARE THE LONELIEST GUYS IN TOWN, they didn't expect us to believe it was literally true. They knew that we'd sympathize with those poor repairmen even though we knew they were fictitious, and that we'd remember their plight.

Advertisers, of course, are notorious for manipulating our emotions to influence our buying decisions. That was the premise of Packard's critique of the "depth approach" to advertising, discussed in the Introduction. The American Express slogan DON'T LEAVE HOME WITHOUT IT exploits the anxiety we experience when traveling. The De Beers slogan DIAMONDS ARE FOREVER plays off our desire for marital fidelity and our fear of or guilt about infidelity. Touting Wheaties as THE BREAKFAST OF CHAMPIONS forges an unlikely connection between wheat flakes and athletic glory. I DREAMED I STOPPED TRAFFIC IN MY MAIDENFORM BRA offers to increase consumers' va-va-voom factor considerably. The name Yahoo! puts a cry of excitement directly into our mouths. The name Monster acknowledges that the search for a job can be overwhelmingly scary.

Emotional appeals are risky. To succeed they either have to be subtle enough to be convincing (like DON'T LEAVE HOME WITHOUT IT), or they have to shoot the moon and be clearly hyperbolic (like THE BREAKFAST OF CHAMPIONS). In between lies dangerous territory where we encounter trite sentimentality, false intimacy, and other perils. CELEBRATE THE MOMENTS OF YOUR LIFE, the General Foods slogan for International Coffees, rings hollow with its bland coziness. Procter & Gamble, the world's largest consumer products company, claims to be TOUCHING LIVES, IMPROVING LIFE. Really? How are you touching my life, P&G? With a Swiffer?

One of the most common ways for an advertiser to get us excited about something is to show us someone else (usually a fictitious character) being excited about it. We're supposed to think, "If that guy is willing to walk a whole mile for a Camel, it must be a really great cigarette!" Here are some slogans that try to inspire infectious enthusiasm:

NOBODY BETTER LAY A FINGER ON MY BUTTERFINGER

I GO CUCKOO FOR COCOA PUFFS!

LEGGO MY EGGO!

I WANT MY MAYPO!

I WANT MY MTV!

M'M! M'M! GOOD *(Campbell Soup)*

Some messages shock us by breaking taboos. In 2008, the teen soap opera *Gossip Girl* got some attention with a series of provocative print and Internet ads. The ads showed the main characters in sexual situations and featured only the following text, in big block letters: "OMFG." (If anyone still needs a translation of this texting abbreviation, it means 'Oh, my fucking god.') There's a certain ingenuity to this ploy—using a convention that's popular with the target demographic of the show to circumvent linguistic and editorial taboos.

There are other, more complex emotional buttons that advertisers have been pushing for a long time. One is a simple sense of self-worth:

YOU DESERVE A BREAK TODAY *(McDonald's)*

BECAUSE I'M WORTH IT *(L'Oréal)*

For the more ambitious, there are messages of self-actualization:

BE ALL THAT YOU CAN BE *(US Army)*

THE POWER TO BE YOUR BEST *(Apple)*

Many slogans offer adventure and escape:

CALGON! TAKE ME AWAY!

FOR PEOPLE WHO SHARE A TASTE FOR EXCITEMENT
(Martini & Rossi)

Some promise to give consumers a certain mystique:

DOES SHE OR DOESN'T SHE? *(Clairol)*

WHO'S THAT BEHIND THOSE FOSTER GRANTS?

Some even become comrades in generational rebellion:

THIS IS NOT YOUR FATHER'S OLDSMOBILE

Book titles also seek to push emotional buttons—especially contemporary books, which enter an unfathomably competitive market. While most people love words and ideas, just mentioning them doesn't really grab someone's attention. The *idea* of an idea is too abstract to be compelling. Books, of course, are full of words and ideas, which means they need spicy titles to attract attention. Here are some recent nonfiction titles:

ADDICTED TO DANGER
NAKED ECONOMICS: UNDRESSING THE DISMAL
    SCIENCE
GOOGLED: THE END OF THE WORLD AS WE
    KNOW IT

The first book is about mountain climbing, so the connection to danger is clear. The other two, however, are about abstract topics. The second title connects eco(yawn)nomics to the titillating topic of nudity. The third implies a link between a search engine company and armageddon—certainly an emotional topic for many people, to say the least.

Perhaps the most insidiously effective emotional appeals concern our relations with other people. We yearn for connection, and when we have it, we invest much of our self-worth in it.

WHEN YOU CARE ENOUGH TO SEND
THE VERY BEST *(Hallmark)*

REACH OUT AND TOUCH SOMEONE *(AT&T)*

MY WIFE, I THINK I'LL KEEP HER *(Geritol)*

That last one, a sweet and folksy sentiment, also manages to work in intimations of mortality.

The mixture of love and guilt experienced by caregivers occupies a category unto itself. The desire to do right by the ones who depend on us runs deep.

UNWRAP A SMILE *(Little Debbie Snack Cakes)*

NO MORE TEARS *(Johnson's Baby Shampoo)*

CHOOSY MOTHERS CHOOSE JIF

DOESN'T YOUR DOG DESERVE ALPO?

Sometimes slogans and jingles try to take the strong feelings we have about important things and transfer them to things that are for sale. One way to do that is to wrap a product in the American flag:

BASEBALL, HOT DOGS, APPLE PIE
AND CHEVROLET

THE GREAT AMERICAN CHOCOLATE BAR *(Hershey's)*

Another way is to get personal:

GRAPES, LIKE CHILDREN, NEED LOVE
AND AFFECTION *(Almaden)*

The point of this last slogan, of course, is to make us believe that Almaden Vineyards takes really good care of its grapes. But there's also the implication that, since the grapes are deserving of such attention, they also deserve our parental love.

Personification—attributing human identities to inanimate objects—is one of the most powerful ways to make an emotional appeal. We're people, and we care about people. We admire them, love them, and sometimes want to be just like them. Personifying products and companies invites us to have emotional relationships with them, and to see human virtues in them, such as loyalty and strength. Brawny paper towels have a big, smiling lumberjack type on their package, turning a boring roll of paper into a friend with a strong back who can help us out in a crisis—even if that crisis is nothing more than spilled milk.

It doesn't take much verbiage to set someone off, and that makes emotional button pushing an effective tool for microstyle.

5

EVOKE SPECIFIC
SITUATIONS

Effective micromessages often call to mind specific situations. There are lots of ways to do that. Chapter 2 discussed frames, which are situations that some words evoke as part of their "portable context." Savvy word choice alone can sometimes surround your message with just the right situation.

But it's more than using specific words. Evoking the complexity and detail inherent in a situation involves telling a story. People who give marketing advice often stress the importance of telling a story, even with a company name. This sounds good, but let's get real—it's hard to actually tell a story in a micromessage. A story has a beginning, a middle, and an end. If your message has fewer than three words, you're screwed. What you *can* do is hint at a story, but your reader will have to flesh it out. The blogger and naming consultant Nancy Friedman expressed this idea well with respect to naming: "Your name is the title of your story, not the story itself."

Let's return to the slogan for Maytag appliances, OUR REPAIR-

MEN ARE THE LONELIEST GUYS IN TOWN. This is a statement, not a story, but it gives you enough information to reconstruct the story, a microtragedy: There are these Maytag repairmen who have trained hard to be able to fix Maytag appliances. They're eager to use their skill and knowledge to help others. Then the tragic twist: the same concern for quality that leads Maytag to have well-trained repairmen also makes Maytag products indestructible. Alas, the poor repairmen never get to use their training. *That's* a story. But the slogan doesn't *tell* it—it merely suggests it.

Why bring up all this stuff about lonely repairmen when you're trying to sell a washing machine? Why be so indirect? First, the idea of the sad repairman adds humor and a human element to what would otherwise be a boring message about reliability. But more important, the specificity of the idea and the way it relates indirectly to reliability are great assets. The relevance principle comes into play: to make the connection between product reliability and a lonely repairman, we construct a story that relates them as cause and effect. Even though we know the story is fictitious, it makes the product attribute seem more real, because we're forced to imagine its consequences.

Some messages that appeal to the senses (see Chapter 3) do so via specific and unusual situations. Think of these slogans:

PLEASE DON'T SQUEEZE THE CHARMIN!

YOU'RE SOAKING IN IT! *(Palmolive dishwashing liquid)*

The first one echoes the old joke of telling someone to stand in a corner and not think of an elephant. You can't help but imagine squeezing the Charmin after you've been told not to. The evoked situation has a lot of detail: you're standing in the grocery store, you grasp the Charmin package in your hands, you feel the soft rolls yielding under the plastic wrapper. It even has an emotional element: you feel slightly embarrassed, and maybe get a bit of a thrill from doing something illicit. The second slogan invites you to imagine the mildness of Palmolive by actually submerging your fingers in it. You feel the goopiness, smell the soapy perfume, see the vivid green.

Sometimes a subtle difference in phrasing can change a simple statement into an implied situation. Consider the following slogan, about Chase bank's ATM machines:

IF THERE'S A CORNER, WE'RE AROUND IT

The slogan might have been "we're around every corner" or even "we're everywhere." Instead Chase uses a more complex conditional construction, with an *if* clause and a consequent clause. The use of the conditional places you in a hypothetical situation. It says, "Imagine you're out walking around. Check to see if there's a corner nearby. If there is, we're around it!" Specific scenarios like this engage the imagination of the reader, even though they're hypothetical.

Advertising often invites you to imagine a specific scenario involving a product. The old Maxwell House Coffee slogan GOOD TO THE LAST DROP makes you think about finishing a cup of coffee and wanting more. Budweiser didn't say, "We make Bud for you," it said THIS BUD'S FOR YOU, as if handing us our own cold bottle. The old FedEx slogan WHEN IT ABSOLUTELY, POSITIVELY HAS TO BE THERE OVERNIGHT makes you remember the desperation of a looming deadline. DOES SHE OR DOESN'T SHE, a slogan written for Clairol in 1955 by Shirley Polykoff, the only female copywriter at Foote, Cone & Belding at the time, relates to hair color very indirectly using a hypothetical scenario of gossip. Because the topic of the gossip is unstated, however, the slogan is ripe for interpretation as a double entendre as well.

Brand names for products sometimes evoke especially exotic

places in which the products might be used—at least in consumers' imaginations. The North Face, which makes outdoor gear, lets chilly urban bus riders imagine they're braving the elements on the exposed face of a mountain. Patagonia lets those same consumers battle an Antarctic chill in Tierra del Fuego. London Fog helps businessfolk from Middle America imagine they're cutting a mysterious figure in the British metropolis (even though, as a British character in *Mad Men* points out, London doesn't even get foggy).

Specific scenarios can also make people laugh. Here's a tweet by @Bcompton quoted in the book *Twitter Wit* (the @ symbol in *@Bcompton* indicates a Twitter user name):

Once I start tooting the empty beer bottles, it's like, TOOT TOOT, HERE COMES THE PARTY BARGE! But then I look around and I'm alone and sad.

Sometimes, alas, specific scenarios lead to unintended humor. Some situations can be evoked well with a single phrase or sentence, and others cannot. Consider this tagline for the movie *The Day of the Dolphin*, another one to make it onto the *Huffington Post*'s "worst ever" list:

UNWITTINGLY, HE TRAINED A DOLPHIN TO KILL THE
PRESIDENT OF THE UNITED STATES.

Reasonable minds might differ about the virtues of the movie itself, but the tagline is just too specific and implausible—it promises humor, not suspense.

One of the best ways to make a message engaging is to make your reader live it, not just think it. And we don't live ideas, we live situations. So, insert your reader into a situation.

6

ZOOM IN ON
TELLING DETAILS

You can never tell the whole story. It doesn't matter whether you're writing a hundred-thousand-page novel or a ten-word tweet. Telling a story, even just communicating a message, always involves deciding what to leave out. Reading a story or understanding a message always requires connecting some dots.

To connect dots, people make inferences based on what they're told, what they know, and what they can figure out from context. The richness of the meaning people derive from a message depends on the possibilities suggested by the details they're given and the situation at hand.

The shorter the message, the more telling those details need to be. Let's return to the probably apocryphal Hemingway story for a moment:

For sale: baby shoes, never used.

This little story has legs. Let's unpack it to see how the details suggest a bigger picture. Most striking are those baby shoes. Since they were never used, we can infer that a baby was expected but isn't on the scene. Was the baby stillborn or lost in a miscarriage? Put up for adoption? Was there a divorce or other estrangement that led the baby to be in the custody of someone other than the owner of the shoes? Were the shoes presented as a reconciliation gift by an absent father and rejected? The questions raised by the shoes are endless, and all the possible answers are heartbreaking. Then there's the "for sale" part. Why would someone sell baby shoes rather than just giving them away? The person who owns these shoes must be really broke. A teenage runaway, perhaps, who planned to keep her baby but put it up for adoption instead?

Many of the six-word memoirs that have been inspired by this story use details to hint at a whole life story. Here's one by Heather Thomas that appeared in the book *Not Quite What I Was Planning*:

Head in books, feet in flowers.

Using little details to stand for bigger events and situations isn't just for verbal messages, of course. The technique occurs often in movies: We know a terrible crime has occurred when we see blood trickling into the gutter. A kiss serves as PG shorthand for an X-rated encounter. The simple gesture of opening a door tells us that a straying lover has been forgiven.

Students in film classes learn that there are two basic and opposed cinematic styles or techniques: montage and mise-en-scène. *Montage* makes meaning out of the juxtaposition of images, one after another. It tells stories using little pieces. *Mise-en-scène* lets the action unfold in detail in front of the camera in long takes. Orson Welles was known for his use of mise-en-scène, and Sergei Eisenstein for his use of montage. A director using montage has to rely on the suggestiveness of individual details to move a story along.

Various academic concepts explore this way of making meaning. Cognitive linguists use the general term *metonymy*, borrowed from classical rhetoric, to describe the real-world relations that allow for inferential and referential connections between concepts. These relations can be physical (as in part-whole relations), situational (as in the relation between customers and their orders in a restaurant), or causal (as in the relation between footprints and the person or animal that made them). When we say to someone, "Get your butt over here!" we expect the rest of the person to come as well. We regularly refer to works of art using the name of the artist who created them, as in "They own three Picassos." Servers in a restaurant often refer to customers by their orders: "The cheeseburger at table three needs a water." In all these cases, we use concepts that are linked in people's minds, using one to stand for the other. In Peirce's semiotic theory, these relations are examples of indexical representation, one of the three main ways in which one thing can stand for another (along with iconic symbolic representation).

Metaphor, discussed in the next chapter, and metonymy (or indexicality), the topic of this chapter, correspond to two even broader ways we have of establishing mental connections between things in the world. On the one hand, we relate things by virtue of perceived similarities or detailed analogical correspondences between them. Images, similes, metaphors, and analogies all fall into this category. On the other hand, we relate things by virtue of real connections between them in time and space. These two broad categories of relations aren't mutually exclusive. Photographs and footprints are based on both similarity and contiguity: they're iconic because they resemble what they represent, and they're indexical because they're caused by what they represent.

Following the terminology of the cognitive linguists, I'll use the general term *metonymy* to refer to phenomena that are connected in these ways. Metonymy is part of how we think. It's part of our memory. For example, we might remember the number of students in a class by picturing the seating arrangement, with each full seat representing a student.

Creative writing classes teach us that, even in verbal communication, showing is often better than saying. Showing something with words means using the right details to make its general characteristics apparent. Instead of saying that a landscape is beautiful, describe it in a way that makes it beautiful in the reader's mind. Metonymy provides one of the best ways to show rather than say. Here's a quote from a talk given by Simon Dumenco, *Ad Age*'s Media Guy, at the Ad Age Digital Conference, April 14, 2010:

> *I've seen the future and it's covered in greasy fingerprints.*

This is a great sound bite—a line from Dumenco's speech that's meant to be remembered and repeated. It uses a specific and vivid detail about the iPad to highlight the new clout the device gave Apple in the media business, and to make a prediction about the types of computing devices that will prove popular with consumers. The reference to greasy fingerprints echoes the one common complaint people made about the device after its debut, when it garnered mostly adoration. Because this image is so memorable, though, it's an example of saying the wrong thing in the right way (see Chapter 9). The fingerprints point to what makes the device exciting: its large, multitouch interface, which enables people to perform a variety of tasks on the screen using gestures that involve more than one finger, such as pinching and twisting.

The name Unbox, for a digital movie download service from Amazon, focuses on a small, literally descriptive detail—the idea or image of a movie being taken out of a box—and uses it to stand for a much larger scenario: a distribution system that's freed from the constraints of physical distance and scarcity. When Herbert Hoover promised A CHICKEN IN EVERY POT, A CAR IN EVERY GARAGE in his 1928 election campaign, he wasn't just talking about cars and chickens. He was talking about prosperity for everyone. Capitol One's question WHAT'S IN YOUR WALLET? uses a physical detail that we all experience to evoke a more complex financial situation (and it manages to work a sexual innuendo in there as well).

In their book *Made to Stick*, Chip and Dan Heath write that stories are more believable when they include some very specific details. As one case, they cite research that found jurors to be significantly more likely to accept lawyers' arguments when those arguments contain some vivid details, even if those details are completely irrelevant to the case. For example, jurors deliberating on a child custody case were told that a mother made her son brush his teeth every night before bed. The study showed that they were more likely to award custody to the mother when they learned that the child used a *Star Wars* toothbrush.

Slogans often present specific details about products and companies from which we infer more general qualities. When Ball Park told us its sausages PLUMP WHEN YOU COOK 'EM, it was showing us, not telling us, how moist and succulent the sausages are. The slogan WHEN E. F. HUTTON TALKS, PEOPLE LISTEN showed us that E. F. Hutton was worth listening to (the company was sold after nearly collapsing during the 1987 stock market crash). Describing Kentucky Fried Chicken as FINGER LICKIN' GOOD made us believe in the greasy tastiness by compelling us to imagine it all over our hands.

Recall from Chapter 2 the way words introduce frames—clusters of background knowledge that put word meanings into context. Choosing the wrong way to indirectly evoke an idea can result in bad framing. The name StubHub, for a website where people buy and sell tickets, uses the word *stub* to stand for tickets. A stub, however, is what's left of a ticket that's already been used.

This metonymy only exacerbates the anxiety people might feel about buying tickets from the strangers who originally purchased them. The name Verb for Shoe uses the word *verb* to represent the dynamic nature of computerized "smart shoes." This metonymy gets points for being unusual, but it lacks punch because it uses a dry, abstract idea to stand for a concrete, interesting one.

In 2010, I saw a billboard for 7-Eleven with the following slogan:

STUFF YOUR FACE WITH VALUE

Pictured on the billboard were two pale, unappealing lumps that I believe were microwavable burritos. That was the "value" you were supposed to stuff in your face. This ad might appeal to people who enjoy taking their meals at 7-Eleven, but it certainly doesn't appeal to me. Part of the reason stems from its peculiar use of metonymy. The word *value* refers to the food items that can be had at 7-Eleven. Tangible food is represented by the concept of the economic value you enjoy when you purchase it. But value, while desirable, lacks both specific sensory associations and emotional appeal.

Usually we use metonymy to make something easier to picture or to understand with our other senses. Representing the concrete in terms of the abstract works only when the abstract concept is especially interesting or emotionally powerful. A slogan like "have a bite of love" might work, because love is, metaphorically speaking, delicious. Value isn't. Taking something that really isn't delicious to begin with, and representing it with a dry, abstract concept like "value," manages to make those burritos look worse, especially since the abstract concept focuses on how little you pay for them.

Then of course there's the expression "stuff your face." It implies getting an excess of food into your stomach as quickly as possible without enjoying it. Overall, this slogan says, "Don't concern yourself with actual pleasure. Just eat some cheap crap and get it over with." Maybe this ad acknowledges the fact that people usually don't eat at 7-Eleven because they *want* to.

With metonymy, you can use a specific object to represent a whole class of objects. The store Staples sells staples, but it also sells the whole range of office supplies (and the word *staples* is also used in this name to mean 'basic needs').

In titles, objects can also stand for elaborate stories in which they figure. Consider movie and book titles such as *The Tin Drum, Top Hat, Full Metal Jacket, She Wore a Yellow Ribbon,* and *The Maltese Falcon*; and titles of TV shows such as *The Wire*. Other types of details make good titles as well. Think of TV shows such as *Six Feet Under,* and movies such as *The Color of Money* and *The Thirty-Nine Steps*.

One specific type of metonymy is *synecdoche*—using parts to represent wholes. When people talk about having a lot of "mouths" to feed or about counting "heads" or giving someone a "hand," they're using synecdoche. Movie titles like *Jaws* and *Faces* and *Claire's Knee* use synecdoche to stand for characters, and they use the characters to stand for the stories they're involved in. Times and specific events can also represent stories, as in *High Noon, The Last Picture Show,* and *The Last Metro*. Locations can too, as in *The Bridge on the River Kwai, California Suite,* and *Paris, Texas*.

Well-chosen details can help you get your message across without spelling it out. They're an invaluable tool of microstyle.

7

TAP INTO METAPHOR

In school, what many of us learn about metaphor is just about the least interesting thing you can say about it: a metaphor is when you say one thing *is* another thing, and a simile is when you say one thing is *like* another thing. That's the kind of factoid that's easy to put on a test but doesn't shed any light. But even as far as it goes, it's not a very accurate or useful characterization of metaphor, because a metaphor can be implicit or even nonverbal, and when it's made explicit, it need not involve an actual statement of equivalence.

Metaphor isn't primarily a matter of words. Metaphor is a conceptual phenomenon, and words just happen to be useful for creating metaphor. The French anthropologist Claude Lévi-Strauss famously quipped that plants and animals are not only good to eat (*bonnes à manger*) but also good to think (*bonnes à penser*). The way we structure our ideas about the natural world helps us organize our thoughts about more complicated matters, such as social relations. In fact, many things—not just plants and animals—are easy to think about, or "good to think," and many others are hard to think about. That's why we have metaphor. It brings big concepts down to a manageable scale. It makes the abstract real and the complex simple. Metaphor enables us to use ideas that are easy to think about as a way to understand more difficult ideas.

Things that are easy to think about are usually things we can understand with the help of our bodies in real time—things we can see, hear, feel, smell, taste, interact with, and have immediate emotional responses to. Things that are hard to think about, such as democracy or truth, are more complicated and abstract. Sometimes they involve complex, hidden causal mechanisms that work over long periods of time in mysterious ways.

Let's use the terminology of cognitive linguistics and call the easier idea the *source*, and the harder idea the *target*. We use the source as a model to structure our thoughts about the target. Explicit similes, such as "life is like a box of chocolates," and analogies, such as "elbow is to arm as knee is to leg," work the same way.

In the *Poetics*, Aristotle said that having a firm grasp on metaphor was the most important aspect of good style. We all use metaphor. It's one of the most powerful meaning shortcuts. It's used in micromessages running the gamut from deep moral proverbs to flippant jokes:

> *An eye for an eye makes the whole world blind.*
> —*Mahatma Gandhi*

> *A squirrel is just a rat with a cuter outfit.*
> —*Carrie Bradshaw (played by Sarah Jessica Parker)*
> *in* Sex and the City

Metaphor adds vividness and pith to everyday speech and to political oratory and slogans, among other things. Abraham Lincoln's well-known reelection campaign slogan from 1864 was

DON'T SWAP HORSES IN MIDSTREAM. He used it during the Civil War to warn us of the dangers of making a change when conditions are turbulent. Republican strategists echoed the phrase during George W. Bush's reelection campaign of 2004, which took place during the Iraq War: DON'T CHANGE HORSES IN MIDSTREAM. This use of the slogan was often parodied as "Don't change horsemen in midapocalypse."

Metaphor can also solve marketing problems. Consider the challenge faced by the founder of an esoteric technology company. Marketing the company means making the technology interesting and accessible to people who don't understand it. Nova Spivack has dealt with that challenge. According to his bio on TypePad, he's a "technology visionary" with "a long-time interest in cognitive science, artificial intelligence, emergent computation, knowledge management and the emerging Semantic Web." He put those heady interests to work by starting a company based on Semantic Web technology, a collection of markup formats and techniques for representing and manipulating the content of web documents. Unfortunately, hardly anyone really knows what the Semantic Web is.

How do you market a company like this to people who aren't web developers or "technology visionaries," or even especially tech savvy? Spivack hired the branding agency Igor to answer that question. Igor proposed naming the company after a crude, mundane product that you probably have in your car trunk, and Twine was born. The name Twine offers a great example of metaphor at work. Twine is really easy to think about. Everyone knows what it is and what it's used for: tying things together. And that's all that most people need to know about Twine the company: it ties together knowledge that people find and share on the web.

Metaphor is a great way to appeal to the senses (see Chapter 3). Since evolution has given us brains that deal first and foremost with the physical world, most ideas that are easy to think about are related to our physical experience. When we think about twine, we recall its rough texture and the way it feels to tie it. Those memories act as brightly colored labels that make our knowledge of the function of twine salient and memorable.

Pageflakes is another good example of the explanatory power of metaphor. This is the name for a web service that lets you create your own home page by arranging little boxes of web content as you wish. The surprising metaphor used in this name helps people understand something about the interface: you drag the little boxes of content around, and where you drop them they stick. They're like flakes. You might also put them in front of you first thing in the morning (like a breakfast cereal).

When names are metaphorical (Twine, Apple, Amazon, Flock, Pluck, Twitter, digg, Adaptive Path, and StumbleUpon are a few examples), there's typically no language to cue any particular target domain. The words used in these names evoke source domains only, merely implying the metaphorical correspondence to the target domain. We have to figure it out from context.

Movie titles, of course, are often metaphorical. The title *The Asphalt Jungle* explicitly maps out a metaphor that treats the urban environment as the wild. *The Big Chill* evokes a loss of passion and idealism. *Sunset Boulevard* is the name of a street but also about the end of a life.

Metaphor clearly isn't just a fancy literary trope used by poets and novelists. It's everywhere; it structures our thoughts, and our normal speech is filled with metaphorical expressions. A classic book about this idea is George Lakoff and Mark Johnson's *Metaphors We Live By*, originally published in 1980. Anyone interested in language should read it.

Metaphors We Live By inspired a cottage industry of linguists who busily examine the role metaphor plays in everyday language and thought. One big idea to emerge from this research asserts that there are really two kinds of metaphor. One involves

clearly different domains of experience and imaginative equiva-
lences between elements of those domains. The slogan DON'T SWAP
HORSES IN MIDSTREAM requires us to think of the president as a
horse that we shouldn't dismount, though outside the context
of the metaphor there's no relevant relation between horses and
presidents. The old Yellow Pages slogan LET YOUR FINGERS DO THE
WALKING relies on a chance similarity between legs walking and
fingers flipping through a book. The slogan FRESH SQUEEZED GLA-
CIERS, for Adelma Mineral Waters, casts the glaciers as fruit, just
because they're both sources of liquid we drink. Metaphors like
these often have a coincidental quality.

Then there's a second, subtler form of metaphor based on correspondences that we experience directly. This kind of metaphor
is so basic that we sometimes don't recognize it as metaphor. Consider the spatial metaphor we use to talk about time when we say
things like, "Summer is coming" or "Summer is fast approaching" or "Summer will soon be here." While summer can't actually approach in the spatial sense, we recognize a deep experiential
correspondence between time and space. The main way we experience time is by observing motion—of the sun across the sky, the
hands around the face of a clock. When we see a vehicle approaching, we anticipate a future event of arrival, and we predict the
time of that arrival from how fast the vehicle is traveling.

Joe Grady, a principal at the consulting firm Cultural Logic,
calls this kind of metaphor *primary metaphor* and wrote a dissertation showing just how important it is. Primary metaphors pervade
our language and thoughts, and provide conceptual shorthand
that crops up all the time in micromessages. The political sound
bite NO CHILD LEFT BEHIND, the company name Adaptive Path, the
news cliché "peace talks move forward," and Herbert Hoover's
1932 campaign slogan, WE ARE TURNING THE CORNER, all use a
metaphor in which improvement or "progress" appears as forward
motion. This metaphorical notion wasn't invented by the authors

of these expressions. It's woven into our language and into the way we think about things, and it's based on the correlation we experience between moving forward and making an effort with a particular objective in mind. When we travel, our goals literally are spatial destinations, and progress toward our goals is physical progress. When we're not moving, we still think and talk about our goals that way (in fact, it's difficult to talk about goals in any other way). Nissan employed a related metaphor in one of its slogans: LIFE IS A JOURNEY. ENJOY THE RIDE.

When AT&T tells us to REACH OUT AND TOUCH SOMEONE, it draws on a powerful primary metaphor that treats emotional intimacy as physical closeness. Part of the power of the metaphor comes from its role in our early experience and our development. As infants and small children, we experience intimacy primarily when we're held. Though we later learn to express intimacy in other ways, the primary experience of it never leaves us, and that experience colors the way we think about intimacy throughout our lives. When Allstate Insurance says YOU'RE IN GOOD HANDS, it uses the primary metaphor that treats protection as physical support.

Grady identified many primary metaphors in his research. Here's a list of them taken from his dissertation:

AFFECTION IS WARMTH

IMPORTANT IS BIG

HAPPY IS UP

INTIMACY IS CLOSENESS

BAD IS STINKY

DIFFICULTIES ARE BURDENS

MORE IS UP

CATEGORIES ARE CONTAINERS

SIMILARITY IS CLOSENESS

LINEAR SCALES ARE PATHS

ORGANIZATION IS PHYSICAL STRUCTURE

HELP IS SUPPORT

TIME IS MOTION

STATES ARE LOCATIONS

CHANGE IS MOTION

ACTIONS ARE SELF-PROPELLED MOTIONS

PURPOSES ARE DESTINATIONS

PURPOSES ARE DESIRED OBJECTS

CAUSES ARE PHYSICAL FORCES

RELATIONSHIPS ARE ENCLOSURES

CONTROL IS UP

KNOWING IS SEEING

UNDERSTANDING IS GRASPING

SEEING IS TOUCHING

People do occasionally create new metaphors, but usually lurking behind them are primary metaphors that we all share and understand. The specific correspondence that Igor set up between twine and the Semantic Web is novel. But we all recognize the deeper metaphor, the correspondence between cognitive connections and physical ones (Grady calls this metaphor "Organization is physical structure"). When we talk about mental experience, we often reference this metaphor—for example, "I had never made that connection before" or "I wasn't able to put the pieces together."

Some theorists suggest that metaphor has been "built in" to the human mind by evolutionary processes. Ray Jackendoff, professor of philosophy and codirector of the Center for Cognitive Studies at Tufts University, has floated the hypothesis that the cognitive structures humans evolved to manipulate and move around in the physical world eventually were repurposed and became the basis for abstract thought. That would explain why spatial metaphors are ubiquitous in human languages.

When they first become aware of the prevalence of metaphor in their everyday speech, some people have a sort of *Matrix* moment. Like Keanu Reeves in the 1990s sci-fi classic, they wonder how far down it goes. And it goes pretty far down. These deep metaphors form a network of underground springs that sustain our conceptual lives. A single word in the right context can tap into this network.

Metaphor is a staple of microstyle because it packs a lot of idea into a little message. It also adds vividness to otherwise drab messages. Both qualities make it a favorite technique of headline writers, who strive to rope in readers with just a few words. Here's a headline that appeared shortly after President Obama took office:

REPUBLICANS STRAIN TO RIDE TEA PARTY TIGER

Let's consider how this might have been worded without the metaphor:

REPUBLICANS TRY TO BENEFIT FROM EXCITEMENT
ABOUT TEA PARTY, BUT IT'S DIFFICULT

This metaphor-less headline is less likely to make someone buy that copy of the *New York Times* they see at the newsstand. The metaphorical headline is both more compact and more interesting. There's something irresistible about the image of a senator in a blue suit hanging on for dear life on a tiger's back.

Sometimes ideas are used literally and metaphorically at the same time:

HAITI'S AFTERSHOCKS FELT AT A SCHOOL IN NEW YORK

This headline appeared after the 2010 earthquake that killed tens of thousands of people in Haiti. As with many quakes, geological aftershocks were a major concern because they caused damaged buildings to collapse, injuring and killing people and interfering with rescue efforts. The aftershocks that were felt in New York, though, were of the metaphorical kind: grief and other consequences for Americans who had lost loved ones in Haiti.

Because metaphor is such a powerful tool of expressive economy, it's often used in six-word memoirs. The following two memoirs draw on the ubiquitous "life is a journey" metaphor:

> *I've never fallen, only slipped.*
> *—SomethingNew, March 13, 2010,*
> *from the Smith Magazine website*

> *Slow lane. Fast lane. Hard shoulder.*
> *—Alex Hansen Today, quoted on the website*
> *for the BBC radio show* Today

I like the specificity of the metaphor used in this memoir:

> *I photoshop people in my head.*
> *—Abigail_Pope, January 31, 2008*

You get the idea that Photoshop functions metonymically here as well—perhaps the author is a photographer or graphic designer. But mostly it acts as a very vivid metaphor for the way we sometimes idealize the people in our lives.

Metaphor can create complexity that's hard to achieve with more direct modes of expression:

> *My parents should've kept their receipt.*
> *—SarahBeth, February 28, 2010*

There's a delicious ambiguity to this memoir; it's hard to know whether to read it as a confession or a condemnation. It implies that the author is damaged goods, but also seems to accuse the parents of crass materialism—what kind of people would return their own child?

A good metaphor leads people to make the inferences you want them to make. From the name Twine we infer that Spivack's Semantic Web technology is useful and easy to use. Those are simple messages, but important ones. The political sound bite NO CHILD LEFT BEHIND implies that we're making progress with our education policy.

So what's a bad metaphor? One that either leads to undesirable inferences, or fails to illuminate the target. Undesirable inferences emanate from the retail outlet name The Dress Barn. This name treats a store, metaphorically, as a place that houses animals. Questions immediately arise: Are the animals the dresses, or the customers? Certainly no dress shopper wants to be described as a cow, horse, goat, or pig. Nor does one want to be wearing a barn animal, or a dress as big as a barn. Barns are about as far from the urbane world of fashion as a place can get, and they stink. The name The Dress Barn is a metaphorical travesty.

Part of the problem with the name BookGoo, besides the unpleasantly evocative sensuousness, is the fact that it seems to use the word *goo* metaphorically, but the metaphor doesn't really help us understand the purpose of the site.

Another bad metaphor name is The Pin Cushion, for an acupuncture clinic in Seattle. We stick pins into pincushions carelessly. Pins don't even have to be very sharp to go into a pincushion. What the namers in this case were going for, presumably, was an image of relaxation: the logo shows a human figure lying back on a pillow. Instead they created an image of carelessness.

Often we're told not to mix metaphors, but metaphors are in fact mixed all the time to great effect. This happens because metaphors are recycled. Ernest Hemingway wrote a story whose title, "Big, Two-Hearted River," treated the river as a living creature with internal organs. In his *New York Times* review of Richard Holmes's book *The Age of Wonder*, Christopher Benfey borrowed Hemingway's title for the opening line: "In this big two-hearted river of a book, the twin energies of scientific curiosity and poetic invention pulsate on every page." Here a book is metaphorically compared to a river, which is metaphorically understood to have two hearts.

Metaphor usually involves a kind of implicit comparison. Sometimes micromessages make their comparisons more explicit. Consider the following slogans:

IT TASTES LIKE A CHOCOLATE MILKSHAKE, ONLY
CRUNCHY! *(Cocoa Krispies)*

THE CHAMPAGNE OF BOTTLED BEER *(Miller beer)*

THE OTHER WHITE MEAT *(National Pork Board)*

The book title *Motherhood Is the New MBA* uses a similar approach. It's interesting to think about whether statements like these count as metaphor, in the conceptual sense, and if they don't, why not. The pork slogan THE OTHER WHITE MEAT seems to be a genuine attempt to include pork, literally, in the category of white meat, along with poultry. The slogan isn't intended as a metaphor, but skeptics might consider it one—and a far-fetched one at that.

Simple metaphors can cast a new light on familiar ideas, and make unfamiliar ones less so. Tapping into the deep network of existing metaphors can activate rich patterns of reasoning.

6

USE AMBIGUITY FOR GOOD, NOT EVIL

May all your love be true love, and all your pain be champagne.

—WEDDING TOAST

Ambiguity can go either way. Its effects range from the ridiculous to the sublime. On the ridiculous end of the spectrum are examples like "Touch Me, I'm Dick," the name of a song written by the rock star wannabe played by Matt Dillon in the 1992 movie *Singles*. The movie takes place in Seattle in the heyday of grunge. The song's fictional title plays on "Touch Me, I'm Sick," the name of an actual song by Mudhoney, one of the representative bands of that scene.

Then there's the sublime end of the scale. In 1978, the ad agency Saatchi & Saatchi created a poster that helped put the Tories and Margaret Thatcher in power in the United Kingdom the following year. It showed a long line of people waiting at the unemployment office under the slogan LABOUR ISN'T WORKING. However you might feel about Thatcher, you have to admit that's a great slogan. One ad industry trade magazine voted it the best ad poster of the twentieth century.

Pressing words into double duty can help you get a lot of meaning out of a little message. If you can find a word or phrase that's ambiguous in just the right way, you get two meanings for the price of one. Puns, double entendres, and many jokes rely on ambiguity. For some people, the perfect double meaning is the holy grail of verbal cleverness. But if you don't take control of ambiguity, it can bite you in the ass.

What distinguishes good from bad ambiguity? As David St. Hubbins (played by Michael McKean) says in the movie *This Is Spinal Tap*, "It's such a fine line between stupid and clever."

For starters, clever ambiguity is always intentional. Most style guides tell us to avoid ambiguity in our writing, and with good reason: it often happens by accident, and when it does, it can undermine our communicative intent, sometimes with comical results. Perhaps the best examples of ambiguity gone wrong are the newspaper headlines known as "crash blossoms." The name comes from one such headline:

VIOLINIST LINKED TO JAL CRASH BLOSSOMS

You might be scratching your head wondering what a "crash blossom" is. If so, you've interpreted this headline in the wrong way (which is hard not to do). The intended meaning is that a violinist whose parents died in a Japan Airlines crash is blossoming—that is, enjoying professional success.

Linguists call this kind of sentence a "garden path" sentence, based on the old expression "to lead someone up the garden path," meaning 'to mislead someone.' Garden path sentences seem to come to an end before they're actually finished. We read along until we come to a word or phrase that appears to complete the meaning of one we've already seen. In the headline above, "crash" seems to complete the meaning of "linked to," and the sentence should be done. But since we see "blossoms" there, we look for the nearest hook to hang it on and combine it with the noun "crash" to yield the fanciful compound "crash blossom."

The classic example that burgeoning linguists encounter in their introductory syntax classes is "The horse raced past the barn fell." Some people have trouble even seeing how this could possibly be a grammatical sentence. The word *raced* seems to be the main verb of the sentence but is actually a past participle modifying *horse*—as in "the horse that was raced past the barn." The word *fell*, which seems to have no business in the sentence, is in fact the main verb.

Another classic linguistic example of ambiguity is "Visiting relatives can be boring." This can mean either 'It is boring to visit relatives,' or 'Relatives who are visiting are boring.' An actual headline from the *Charlotte Observer*, April 9, 2010, read, HOME CRUSHED BY TREE WITH DOG INSIDE. Here the ambiguity is in the prepositional phrase "with dog inside"; the dog seems to be inside the tree, but it's supposed to be inside the house.

Sometimes ambiguity involves an incorrect interpretation that's even more comically absurd. Consider the following:

GRANDMOTHER OF EIGHT MAKES HOLE IN ONE

PROSTITUTES APPEAL TO POPE

IRAQI HEAD SEEKS ARMS

RED TAPE HOLDS UP NEW BRIDGE

YOU CAN PUT PICKLES UP YOURSELF

MCDONALD'S FRIES THE HOLY GRAIL FOR
POTATO FARMERS

Headlines like these have been circulating for so long without attribution that it's hard to tell whether they actually appeared in newspapers or were just made up for laughs. Either way, they're hilarious.

Unintentional ambiguity doesn't afflict only headlines. In their book *The Age of Persuasion*, admen Terry O'Reilly and Mike Tennant report seeing the following slogans:

AT PRICES LIKE THESE, OUR APPLIANCES
WON'T LAST LONG!

PANTIES AND BRAS, HALF OFF!

The first one is truly a howler. The second can really go either way. If it's unintentional, it's hilarious. If it's intentional, it's still hilarious, but also rather clever. And racy. When I walked past a local community college campus, I saw this slogan on a poster for a used-textbook website:

BUY EARLY, GET USED

I guess customers can't say they weren't warned.

Sometimes ambiguity is played for laughs. Comedians often build jokes around ambiguous phrases and sentences. This was one of Groucho Marx's favorite techniques:

I shot an elephant in my pajamas. How he got in my pajamas, I'll never know.

Outside of a dog, a book is a man's best friend. Inside of a dog, it's too dark to read.

These jokes use ambiguous prepositional phrases. In the first joke, it's not clear whether "in my pajamas" modifies "I" or "an elephant." In the second, the prepositional phrase "outside of a dog" can be interpreted to mean 'other than a dog,' or it can be taken literally.

During the 2008 presidential election, during which Barack Obama made the idea of change his campaign theme, the *Onion* played on stereotypes to cast him as a panhandler in the following ambiguous headline:

BLACK GUY ASKS NATION FOR CHANGE

The kind of ambiguity in the preceding headlines is embarrassing because it leads to interpretations that are unintended and often absurd or highly inappropriate. But the kind of ambiguity we see in LABOUR ISN'T WORKING seems like magic. Somehow, if you manage to craft a message that delivers two equally natural and appropriate meanings simultaneously, it's as if the language itself supports the truth and wisdom of what you're saying.

Clever ambiguity involves meanings that are clearly distinct, equally natural with the same pronunciation, and equally appropriate to the situation. LABOUR ISN'T WORKING succeeds on all counts. The two interpretations of this slogan—that workers don't have jobs, and that the Labour Party isn't performing well—are clearly distinct: one is about citizens, and the other is about their government. These two meanings are conveyed with the same pronunciation, and they're both eminently relevant to an election: one describes a pain felt by voters, and the other describes the implied cause.

Advertising slogans often strive for clever ambiguity and sometimes hit the mark. The old slogan for Gillette razor blades, THE BEST A MAN CAN GET, manages to simultaneously tout the quality of the company's blades and promise self-actualization to its customers. For a while Viagra used the slogan LOVE LIFE AGAIN, which can imply a return of one's sex life or of one's joie de vivre—or, of course, both. The GE slogan WE BRING GOOD THINGS TO LIFE means both 'we make good things come alive' and 'we add good things to life.' The New York City mattress store Sleepy's uses the slogan FOR THE REST OF YOUR LIFE, which promises both refreshing sleep and long-lasting products.

Headline writers sometimes use intentional ambiguity. Health .com ran a story about the health benefits of coffee with the headline THE MANY PERKS OF COFFEE. And it's hard to believe that the editors at CNN didn't recognize the ambiguity of this headline from January 1, 2010:

TESTS FIND "NOTHING WRONG" WITH
LIMBAUGH'S HEART

This headline was ostensibly about Limbaugh's cardiac health, not about his capacity for love.

Double meanings are also big in book titles. The recent nonfiction title *The Union of Their Dreams*, about César Chávez's farm worker movement, refers both to an ideal labor union and to all farm workers' hopes and aspirations taken in the aggregate. The title *Street Fighters*, about the final days of Bear Stearns, suggests brawling gangs as well as a fight for survival on Wall Street.

Movie titles, too, often go for double meanings. The 1948 film *A Foreign Affair* is about interpersonal relations as well as international ones. *Swing Time* is about tripping the light fantastic as well as punching the clock. *A Shot in the Dark* is about a murder and also about a bumbling detective trying his best.

For ambiguity to be really good, both interpretations have to be spot-on. If one interpretation doesn't really fit the situation, the message falls flat. A magazine for women lawyers who specialize in litigation is called *Sue*. While this name does have two distinct interpretations, one of them—Sue as a woman's name—is a bit arbitrary. There are so many women's names to choose from that the coincidence of meaning doesn't seem very magical. So this title doesn't really wow.

An intentional ambiguity can also fall flat if the two meanings are not distinct enough. The old slogan THE BEST TIRES IN THE WORLD HAVE GOODYEAR WRITTEN ALL OVER THEM seems pointless because the literal interpretation, the one involving actual words on the tires, doesn't add anything to the message. Idiomatically, this statement means that it's obvious Goodyear is responsible for such great tires, but that's just what the actual words on the tires tell us. Nothing especially clever about that.

Ambiguity is weak when it's based on spelling and not pronunciation. IBM used the slogan WE MAKE IT HAPPEN; but to get the interpretation relevant to "information technology," you have to pronounce "IT" as two letters rather than one word. We can think of this as "eye ambiguity," like "eye rhyme" in poetry, but that makes it seem only moderately more clever.

When one of the meanings of an ambiguous message is racy, we can consider the message a *double entendre* (which means, roughly, 'double meaning' in French). Country music is known for its (often corny) double entendres and puns. Country songwriter David Bellamy wrote this wonderful lyric:

If I said you had a beautiful body would you hold it against me?

He says he heard the line from Groucho Marx on his show *You Bet Your Life*. It plays on the ambiguity of the phrase "hold it against me," which can be interpreted idiomatically to mean 'judge me harshly for it,' but can, of course, also be interpreted literally. In the first case, "it" refers to the speaker's statement, and in the second, "it" refers to the beautiful body in question.

The book *Twitter Wit* featured this tweet by @Fistsoffolly:

Things were going beautifully until he professed his undying non-ironic love for Ronald Reagan. Nothing trickled down tonight, I assure you.

Pretty good, though the economic meaning of "trickle down" isn't especially well motivated here. While it's a reference to the fiscal conservatism of the tweeter's date, only the sexual meaning makes sense in the immediate context of the evening.

Language is filled with ambiguity. This is almost always regarded as one of its more puzzling and problematic properties. In fact, linguistic ambiguity was one of the biggest bugaboos for brainy types throughout the twentieth century. Big-name philosophers such as Gottlob Frege, Bertrand Russell, and Ludwig Wittgenstein were a little obsessed with it. Frege, a founding figure in the modern study of logic and the philosophy of language, was especially hard-core. He got things started, in the later part of the nineteenth century, with the following observation, from his paper "On the Scientific Justification of a Conceptual Notation":

Language proves to be deficient . . . when it comes to protecting thought from error. It does not even meet the first requirement which we must place upon it in this respect; namely, being unambiguous. The most dangerous cases [of ambiguity] are those in which the meanings of a word are only slightly different, the subtle and yet not unimportant variations.

Frege concluded that "we need a system of symbols from which every ambiguity is banned, which has a strict logical form from which the content cannot escape." Russell and Wittgenstein were also troubled by the way linguistic ambiguity could lead philosophers astray. Russell wrote, "The philosopher . . . is faced with the difficult task of using language to undo the false beliefs that it suggests."

Wittgenstein, one of the most influential philosophers of the twentieth century, argued in his first major work, the *Tractatus Logico-Philosophicus*, that all philosophical problems are actually conceptual confusions caused by the imperfect structures of natural human languages such as German and English. One of their major imperfections, in his view, is the fact that a single form can be used with more than one meaning. Wittgenstein expressed concern about the ambiguity both of individual words and of word classes such as intransitive verb, adjective, and noun. He proposed that the task of philosophers is to reveal the conceptual confusions that underlie philosophical questions by translating those questions into a perfect language like the one envisioned by Frege. This perfect language, Wittgenstein suggested, would mirror the logical structure of the universe.

In his later work, Wittgenstein gave up on the idea that everyday language can be replaced by a more perfect language, but he remained concerned about the conceptual confusions that can arise from ambiguity in language.

Philosophers aren't the only ones who have been troubled by ambiguity. For lexicographers, the fact that words have multiple meanings complicates the process of writing dictionary entries. For computer scientists, the existence of multiple interpretations of words and syntactic structures is one of the major obstacles to the automatic analysis of language by computers. For censors, ambiguity threatens to circumvent restrictions on speech through its double meanings. In the 1930s, the Soviet regime attempted to impose "one-meaningness" (*odnoznachnost*) to stamp out the intellectual dangers of ambiguity.

Ambiguity in language has a variety of forms and sources. Some cases of ambiguity have a decidedly coincidental flavor. For example, consider the sentence

I saw her duck.

This can mean either 'I saw her perform the act of ducking' or 'I saw the duck that belongs to her.' The ambiguity between these two readings results from a number of coincidences, most notably the two meanings of the word *her*, which can be either the accusative or the possessive form of the second person singular pronoun in English, and of the word *duck*, which is both a noun that refers to a type of waterfowl, and a verb for a certain action. There's little reason to believe ambiguity like this tells us anything interesting about English or about language in general. While it might pose a problem for a computer, it seldom does for ordinary folks. In an actual conversation, context would almost certainly clear up the meaning of a sentence like this. Wittgenstein observed this when he made the claim that philosophical problems arise when language "goes on holiday"—that is, when it's removed from the meaningful activities or "language games" in which it normally functions.

Because micromessages such as headlines often lack meaningful context, they're another domain, besides philosophy, in which language goes on holiday. When ambiguity arises as a result, it's important to be in control of the itinerary.

9

SAY THE WRONG THING

People are always trying to say the right thing. Try saying the wrong thing instead. Defying expectations can really make others take notice and listen. But you have to do it in the right way, of course. Not just any old wrong thing will do.

You don't have to be outrageous when you say the wrong thing. It's not always a matter of shocking people (though it certainly can be). When Birgitta Jónsdóttir was first elected to the Icelandic parliament in 2009, she produced this nice sound bite: "The good thing about being new in Parliament is not knowing the traditions." This is a nugget of wisdom wrapped in a contradiction, like something Yogi Berra might have said, if he had ever run for the Icelandic parliament. Jónsdóttir's comment seems illogical— as if she's saying it's good that she doesn't know what she's doing. But of course the implication is that there's something wrong with the traditions of the Icelandic parliament and she's not going to be hindered by them. It's her way of saying that she's bringing a new perspective to parliament, but with a little twist that serves as a "brain hook."

Most situations have expectations built right into them. In politics, a party or candidate will always strive to be portrayed in the best possible light. In business, you can be certain that a company will make positive claims about itself or its products or services. That's just part of what it means to engage in those competitive activities. When a message landscape is predetermined in this way, it can lead to an unrelenting sameness. And that, of course, presents a great opportunity to be different.

In politics and business, saying the wrong thing in the right way can't be a simple matter of negative self-presentation. A serious candidate would never make the "blunder," which the *Onion* imaginatively attributed to Barack Obama in the 2008 presidential campaign, of saying "I would make a bad president." The trick is to be backhandedly boastful.

One way to do this is to simply dress up a boast as a confession of weakness. Job candidates are often forced into this strategy in interviews—when asked to identify their own negative qualities, they feel compelled to say something like, "Sometimes I just care too much and work too hard!" A more subtle approach makes a small, seemingly self-critical claim that actually implies something positive and more important. When someone says, "I'm really not much of an athlete," the unspoken message might be "but we both know I'm much smarter than you are."

Some ad campaigns take this tack, making an apparently negative claim that implies a positive one. In fact, one of the most famous ad campaigns of all time, chosen by *Ad Age* magazine as the best campaign of the twentieth century, was the one that Doyle Dane Bernbach created for Volkswagen featuring the slogan THINK SMALL. This slogan inverts the conventional expression "think big," which is supposed to reveal what people need to do to achieve excellence. Was the Volkswagen slogan telling people to settle for mediocrity? No. First, it was getting their attention, and then it was asking them to rethink what's actually important in a car. THINK SMALL put the spotlight on the benefits of economy and fuel efficiency as opposed to power and luxury. Volkswagen also called attention to the odd appearance of its cars with the slogans UGLY IS ONLY SKIN DEEP and WHILE IN EUROPE, PICK UP AN UGLY EUROPEAN. Again, the implication is positive—it's what's inside that counts. (Or, as Gary Shandling once said about a bald character on the *Larry Sanders Show*, "It's the hair inside that counts.")

A clothing designer who presented at Fashion Week 2009 called his collection Bland, which happens to be his middle name. In fashion, this name is counterintuitive in the extreme. But it got noticed—a *New York Times* reporter commented on how funny it was. The name Virgin seems all wrong for an airline, as Nancy Friedman called to my attention—do you really want to fly with someone who has no experience?—but that doesn't prevent the Virgin brand from succeeding. Avis Rent A Car System used to boast, WE'RE NUMBER TWO. WE TRY HARDER, responding to a campaign Hertz ran about being number one. In a similar ploy, Goodrich tires used the slogan WE'RE THE OTHER GUYS to distinguish itself from Goodyear and its famous blimp. Chivas Regal Scotch wore its price tag on its sleeve with the slogan ISN'T THAT A LOT FOR A BOTTLE OF SCOTCH? YES. Listerine focused on effectiveness rather than pleasantness with the slogan THE TASTE YOU HATE TWICE A DAY. While laboring to turn around the troubled Chrysler Corporation in the 1980s, Lee Iacocca used the phrase IF YOU FIND A BETTER CAR, BUY IT! You don't expect to hear the head of a corporation telling you to buy someone else's car.

Some guys in Seattle started an athletic apparel company and called it Lard Butt. The company makes sweatshirts and other items with the name prominently displayed on them. This seems to be a more complicated case, because Lard Butt doesn't really imply anything positive; it's over-the-top negative. But there is a countermessage here—"I don't take myself too seriously"—and it's a refreshing one in the context of sporting goods advertising, which tends to foster earnest fantasies about athletic glory. Embracing a negative term like this can also remove its sting; think of the way the word *queer* has turned from an insult to a label worn with pride.

Grice, the philosopher whose conversational "maxims" we saw in the introduction to these chapters on meaning, recognized that people sometimes violate the rules of conversation intentionally to make a point. He called it "flouting." One way to flout is by damning with faint praise, a violation of Grice's maxim of quantity: "Say enough to be informative, and not more." A classic example is the hypothetical professor who writes a letter of recommendation praising a student for being punctual and having excellent handwriting. The information that's missing from this recommendation—anything that would bear on the student's intellect or other abilities—says more than the information presented.

Saying the wrong thing is a special way to flout Grice's maxim of relation, which says, "Be relevant." This strategy doesn't work in all contexts. It has to be possible to retrieve the positive countermessage. This is the relevance principle at work. Upon encountering an apparently negative claim when only a positive one is expected—in an ad, for example—we keep searching, subconsciously, until we find a positive twist.

Without the background knowledge that carmakers constantly brag about the luxurious interiors and smooth rides of their big tanks (which they did when the Volkswagen slogan came out), and that they always, always want people to like their products, a slogan like THINK SMALL would simply be confusing. You hear it, and then your background mind immediately gets to work, trying to see around the apparently negative claim to the positive message that stands behind it.

Being surprising isn't always so counterintuitive—sometimes it just means zigging when others are zagging. After the collapse of the financial industry in 2008, BECU credit union started using the slogan WE ARE TURNING THE FINANCIAL WORLD RIGHT SIDE UP. This campaign swims against a strong current in advertising that celebrates being unconventional and disruptive. The slogan suggests that the risky methods of modern investment companies have already turned the financial world upside down, and we're learning that's not such a great thing. It promises a comforting return to something more conventional and stable.

Nonfiction book titles sometimes pique interest by straining credulity. Does anyone really believe they can achieve *The 4-Hour Work Week*, or that it's possible to learn *How to Teach Physics to Your Dog?*

When context imposes few expectations, a message can introduce them itself, and then violate them, resulting in a kind of paradox. Titles of movies and books sometimes take this approach. *Back to the Future* is a paradoxical title that brilliantly and compactly evokes the concept of time travel. Notice that a title like "To the Future" doesn't work the same way, because we metaphorically think of time in terms of motion (see Chapter 6)—we can get "to the future" simply by waiting. But "back to the future" is a phrase that would be spoken only by someone who has already been there! Jenny Holzer, a conceptual artist who works with text, produced a series of aphorisms she called *Truisms*. Here's one with a paradoxical flavor:

Playing it safe can cause a lot of damage in the long run.

Here's a paradoxical six-word memoir from the *Smith Magazine* website:

Politician for years rescued by defeat.
　　　　　　　—Frank Howard, January 24, 2008

Miller Lite was once sold with the paradoxical slogan EVERY-THING YOU ALWAYS WANTED IN A BEER . . . AND LESS. The title of one book about the economic difficulties of recent years is *The Value of Nothing.*

Another way to say the wrong thing is to produce what seems like a *tautology*, a statement that's true by definition. Yogi Berra, who had a microstyle all his own, famously quipped, "You can observe a lot just by watching." Woody Allen said, "I don't want to achieve immortality through my work—I want to achieve it through not dying." Similar statements inhabit realms of our language both lofty ("A rose is a rose is a rose is a rose"—Gertrude Stein) and quotidian ("It is what it is").

In some contexts, the unexpected turns into a counterstyle and becomes . . . expected. Band names, especially in particular genres, are like that. Rock or "alternative" music often presents a countercultural point of view in the United States. The very label *alternative* implies this and has mysteriously supplanted the term *rock* even when it refers to work that is unmistakably part of the rock tradition. (At one time *alternative* referred to music that wasn't distributed by big media corporations.) This countercultural stance includes an implied critique of American capitalism. Nevertheless, music fandom reproduces the dynamics of speculative investment. People who embrace a band early in its career often feel they've made a special investment of cultural capital. If the band makes it big, these early fans expect a return on their cultural capital in the form of respect for their credibility or authenticity. Newcomers are regarded with suspicion; their investments might dilute the value of the band's stocks.

Names of punk and heavy-metal bands have long been a genre of antibranding that embraces everything offensive and unappealing: Anthrax, Megadeth, the Sic Fucks, the Dead Kennedys, etc. This naming orthodoxy is nicely parodied by the fictitious band Spinal Tap, which takes its name from an extremely unpleasant medical procedure that nonetheless lacks the sinister, taboo-breaking glamour of references to death, weapons, and the occult.

People create humor with outrageously incongruous statements. After the 2001 attacks on the World Trade Center towers in New York, the *Onion* ran the following headline:

WHAT IS SEXY IN THE WAKE OF SEPT. 11?

This massive tragedy was about the least sexy thing anyone could imagine. The headline worked because it pointed to the vacuity of so much news reporting and its inadequacy for dealing with such an event.

Someone on Twitter came up with this dark take on psychotherapy:

> *Doctor this afternoon: "Ever have thoughts of hurting yourself?" Me: "Nope." Doc: "Any idea why not?"*
> — @krahigail, *quoted in* Twitter Wit

Somehow this bit of imagined dialogue seems perfectly natural, even though the doctor's follow-up question is monstrous in a therapeutic context.

There are many ways to say the wrong thing. Choosing the right way to do it can make a real impact.

SOUND

Evolution involves compromises. One is apparent in the design of the human throat. When we eat, food has to pass over the trachea to travel down the esophagus to the stomach. That makes us more vulnerable than other animals to choking. This design flaw emerged in our species because the configuration enables us to produce a greater range of vocal sounds. We risk choking so that we can speak.

The range of ideas we need to communicate is vast. Therefore, we need large vocabularies, which means we need a large repertoire of speech sounds to distinguish words from one another. Evolution has molded the human vocal tract into a subtle instrument. The voice symbolizes our expressive ability, lays the foundation for our social life, and nurtures the roots of our music.

When you talk, you push air out of your lungs and through your trachea, your larynx, and your vocal cavity. What happens to the air during that journey makes the music of your speech. As the air passes through your larynx, you can tighten your vocal folds so they vibrate. The vibration makes the resonant sound that forms the basis of singing and of vowels, the hearts of syllables. Then your tongue and lips and other parts of your mouth and throat form obstructions that change frequencies in the sound and introduce noisy turbulence and brief silences to the sound to give it a kind of shape. Linguists have created an elaborate phonetic alphabet to represent the sounds of the world's languages in terms of all this complicated machinery.

The voice is really like a musical wind instrument. The vibration of the vocal folds is like the vibration of lips playing a trumpet, or a reed in a clarinet. The size of the space those vibrations traverse determines the pitch range of the instrument, and that size correlates pretty well with body size. Larger people tend to have lower voices, like tubas, trombones, bassoons, or bass clarinets. Smaller people tend to have higher voices, like flutes, trumpets, and soprano saxophones.

The resonant sound of the human voice is composed of different prominent frequencies. The way you change the shape of your vocal tract can raise and lower different prominence peaks, producing the distinct qualities of different vowels. But speech isn't just vowels. Consonants make our speech snap, crackle, and pop. They make it hiss, hum, buzz, and glide. Consonants are like edges. They give language its shape and texture. They can be rounded or angular, hard or soft, smooth or rough. We produce consonants by interrupting the flow of air through the vocal tract in different ways, sometimes completely stopping and releasing it, sometimes creating turbulence, and sometimes warping the overall shape more like we do with vowels.

We measure speech in syllables. A syllable always has a vowel. Consonants are like bookends: they can be placed at one or both ends of a syllable (in English), but they're optional. Most languages with traditional poetic forms base them on syllables. Some forms specify the total number of syllables per line; haiku, for example, has three lines, with five syllables in the first line, seven in the second, and five again in the third. In languages such as English, in which syllables receive different degrees of emphasis, the emphasized syllables play a special role. Some poetic forms are based only on the emphasized syllables. The Old English poem *Beowulf*, for example, consists of paired lines, each containing two emphasized syllables.

Hearing people can't separate a word or phrase from its sound. The sound is a little handle that you use to retrieve a meaning from memory, and it's the bell you ring to awaken that meaning in someone else's mind. Sound is the sensuous part of a word or phrase. When you hear a sound it can be musical or harsh, and when you pronounce a sound it can feel elegant or awkward in your mouth. Even when you read words on a page, you can't help thinking about how they sound and what they feel like to say, because that's an important part of the way they're represented in your mind.

It's important to remember that sound isn't the same thing as spelling. English spelling is supposed to be a way to represent the sounds of language, but for various reasons it's quite imprecise. Part of the problem is that spelling is conservative, while pronunciation is progressive. The spelling of some words, like *though*, hasn't changed for hundreds of years, while our pronunciation has changed enough to make that *gh* on the end a real mystery to most people. Something else that makes our spelling imprecise is the fact that we borrow words from other languages, maintaining the spellings they have in different orthographic systems. So although the letter *l* usually represents one particular sound, as in the word *lemon*, we have words like *tortilla* in which it's used differently.

While meaning is the essence of a message, sound, whether real or imagined, is how a message presents itself. And like it or not, people are superficial: beautiful words often seem truer than ugly ones. Your message will be judged as an aesthetic object. That doesn't just mean you should have a well-tuned instrument;

it also means you should play a good tune. If you strive for poetry in your messages, here are some questions to ask about its sound: Does it have rhythm? Do the sounds make a pleasing pattern? Do they fit the meaning?

In the most general terms, poetic language often just "sounds good" or is "easy to say" or "rolls off the tongue" or "has a nice ring to it," and this quality is important in micromessages. In 2006, Princeton psychologists Adam Alter and Daniel Oppenheimer found that companies whose names and stock ticker symbols are "more pronounceable" perform better in initial public offerings than do those with hard-to-pronounce names and symbols. This correlation, of course, reflects short-term perceptions among investors, not long-term company performance, but still, that's not bad for a few letters, is it?

Chapters 10–13 discuss different ways to make messages easier and nicer to pronounce and hear.

10

KEEP IT SIMPLE

There's nothing complicated about keeping the sound of your message simple. First, it should be easy to figure out what the sound is from the spelling. Second, it should be easy to pronounce. Third, it should be easy to understand when you hear it.

When people talk, they don't want to make more of an effort than necessary. If you're creating a message to be repeated, it's best to embrace people's naturally lazy tendencies. Even if you don't expect your message to be repeated out loud, people will hear it in their heads. A clear, simple sound will make a better impression and be easier to remember.

The first step to making something simple is to make it short. People like nicknames. They'd rather say "Chris" and "Meg" than "Christopher" and "Margaret." They'd rather say "FedEx" than "Federal Express" (or "FedEx Kinko's"), and they prefer "Coke" to "Coca-Cola." (The Coca-Cola company wised up and trademarked "Coke" when it realized people wouldn't give up that nickname.)

Slogans keep it simple by communicating clearly with short, familiar words: I LIKE IKE (Eisenhower); IT'S SO SIMPLE (Polaroid); JUST DO IT (Nike); I'M LOVIN' IT (McDonald's). When slogans get too long, they become hard to say and to remember. Consider PATIENT FOCUSED, CUSTOMER CENTERED, CAREGIVER INSPIRED (American Medical Response) and PERMITTING TRAVEL TO SPACE, TRAVEL IN SPACE, AND TRAVEL THROUGH SPACE (the former slogan of Pioneer Rocketplane).

When you're thinking about making the sound of your message simple, keep in mind the difference between writing and sound. Some complexity is purely orthographic: it's hard to figure out how to pronounce a message based on the spelling. This kind of complexity applies only to coined words (including names) and messages containing obscure vocabulary. For your audience, this is decoding complexity: how to get from the spelling to the sound. In some cases it's hard to assign any pronunciation at all to a written form, as in the names Adapx, Knouen, and Indistr. Other times it's hard to decide between two (or more) possibilities. Should the name Openomy be emphasized on the first, second, or third syllable?

Simple also means easy to pronounce. Some words and phrases roll off the tongue like a buttered marble, while others stick in your mouth like caramel corn. Stephin Merritt, the pop songwriting genius behind the Magnetic Fields and other musical groups, decided not to keep it simple when naming the albums for one of his side project bands called the 6ths (itself a real mouthful). The band's two albums are called *Wasps' Nests* and *Hyacinths and Thistles*. These tongue-twisting names are sort of a practical joke— a radio DJ's nightmare. Just imagine having to announce one of these albums on the air.

Unless you're composing a tongue twister or a joke (and you're as clever as Stephin Merritt), it's best to keep the sounds of your messages simple and appealing. That's largely a matter of avoiding ugly knots of consonants. Think of pronunciation as driving. Vowels are like cruising down the open road. Consonants are like city driving, with all its stops, perilous lane changes, and unexpected turns. Saying "hyacinths and thistles" is like having to cross three lanes of busy traffic to exit the freeway, only to find yourself heading east instead of west.

Real words are coveted as domain names not just because they have meanings, but also because everyone knows how to pronounce and spell them. Many of the best company names are single, simple words: Apple, Amazon, Twitter. When you make up a new sound rather than using one that people already know, it's especially important to make it simple. Contrast the name Kodak, which is easy to pronounce the first time you see it, with the name Knouen. Kodak sticks to a simple spelling formula: one letter per sound. That makes it a picture of orthographic efficiency. Its pronunciation, with alternating consonants and vowels, is a model of phonetic simplicity. It comes close, in fact, to what linguists consider a sort of Platonic ideal of word pronunciations: two syllables, each consisting of one consonant followed by one vowel, represented like this:

CV CV

That's the "preferred" word structure in the world's languages, meaning a toddler or a speaker of any language can easily pronounce a word with that structure. Once you start running together vowels or, especially, piling up consonants, things get more complicated. The title *Wasp's Nests* looks like this:

CVCCC CVCCC

Schlotsky's (CCVC CCVC) Deli is tough enough for an English speaker to pronounce, but just imagine how hard it is for the poor speaker of Japanese, a language that has almost no adjacent consonants. And not all consonant clusters are created equal. Some names used in English-speaking places start with sound combinations that, while not unpronounceable, are rare or nonexistent in English: Sclipo (a "social learning network"), Srixon (a golf ball manufacturer), Vlingo (a voice-to-text app for mobile devices), and Zlio (a site to instantly create an online affiliate store) are a few examples. People will probably be able to pronounce these, but they'll stumble and feel funny doing it.

Simple means easy to hear, as well as easy to pronounce. The first season of Tina Fey's TV sitcom *30 Rock*, about a fictitious television sketch comedy show not unlike *Saturday Night Live*, had a running gag about an indie movie called *The Rural Juror*. (Try saying that out loud and you'll hear an indistinct aural mush.) Jenna, the insecure former star of the TV show who had been bumped to a supporting role, landed the lead role in the film and clung to it as proof of her talent. Whenever she talked excitedly about the project, the other characters struggled in vain to make out the words in the title, often speculating incorrectly about what they were (*Roar Her, Gem Her? Oral Germ Whore?*).

If your message is brief, has transparent and economical spelling, and has a distinct and easy-to-pronounce sound, then you've done your part to keep it simple.

11

GIVE IT RHYTHM

W/ hy do we say "salt and pepper" rather than "pepper and salt"? Part of the reason is just convention and habit. But why did the convention settle on that pronunciation? Why does "pepper and salt" sound odd? In a word, rhythm.

Language has rhythm. That's the basis for poetry, rap, and song. Some people, in fact, think that language began in our evolutionary history as song and still shares structural features with music. In many traditions music is built around relatively brief units of structure called *phrases*, the length of which are naturally determined by the limits of human breath. These limits are purely practical with some instruments, especially the human voice. When you're singing or playing any kind of wind instrument, you have to pause at regular intervals to take a breath. And this constraint has influenced musical forms, so now most musical works are built around them: even stringed and other nonwind instruments often play in phrases that are roughly as long as a spoken sentence.

Breath imposes a sort of macro level of rhythm on music and on speaking, but spoken language also has rhythm at a finer scale. As we saw in the previous chapter, all languages have syllables, which form a universal foundation for poetic rhythm. In some languages, such as French, traditional poetic forms are based on counting syllables.

English is a stress-accent language, which means it has syllables with different degrees of emphasis. The patterns made by these peaks and valleys of emphasis are what give our language its swing, and they provide the foundation for meter in traditional forms of English poetry. Literary analysts sometimes make meter visible by using "/" for stressed syllables and "x" for unstressed ones. (There are, in fact, different degrees of emphasis, and showing that level of detail can reveal additional complexity in poetic patterns, but the stressed/unstressed distinction is sufficient for most traditional poetic forms.)

Syllable stress analysis enables us to see the patterns we hear. The old cigarette slogan WINSTON TASTES GOOD LIKE A CIGARETTE SHOULD, for example, has a very regular rhythm that's easy to see when it's written out:

/ x x / x x / x x /

We get simple poetic rhythm drilled into our heads at a young age with nursery rhymes and children's stories:

Jack and Jill went up the hill	/ x / x / x /
To fetch a pail of water	x / x / x / x
Jack fell down and broke his crown	/ x / x / x /
And Jill came tumbling after	x / x / x / x
One day making tracks	x / x x /
In the prairie of Prax	x x / x x /

Came a north-going Zax	x x / x x /
And a south-going Zax	x x / x x /

—Dr. Seuss

The rhythm that characterizes poetry also forms a part of normal speech. In "salt and pepper," emphasized syllables alternate with nonemphasized syllables. That's a sort of default rhythm that we fall back on when we're not thinking much about it. It's the path of least resistance, so to speak, for English. The last chapter talked about the "preferred" syllable structure of CV—a consonant followed by a vowel—that exists in the world's languages. *Preferred* in this context means that structure predominates in a number of ways, even though many syllables don't conform to that structure. We tend to produce and preserve the clearest and simplest contrasts in linguistic forms because those contrasts make the forms easy to transmit and receive—they up the signal-to-noise ratio. In syllables, it's the business of consonants and vowels to be different from one another. Vowels give consonants a space in which to be heard. So consonants "like" to be next to vowels. Similarly, in stress-accent languages like English, contrasts between stressed and unstressed syllables are easiest to hear when those syllables occur next to each other, so it's natural for them to alternate. That's why "salt and pepper" sounds more natural than "pepper and salt."

Some rhythms are downright unnatural, though. A Twitter user tried to coin the term *marketrepreneur*, which has three adjacent unstressed syllables in the middle.

/ x x x /

This word pushes our language's preference for alternating syllables to the breaking point, making it hard to pronounce and extremely unnatural sounding, and it simply won't catch on.

That's not to say you always have to create the most natural rhythm for a message. Different rhythms create different moods, and you can use these to support or complement the meanings of your messages.

A very basic rhythmic contrast is the one between two different types of metrical units: *iambs*, which consist of an unstressed syllable followed by a stressed one (dee DUM); and *trochees*, which consist of a stressed syllable followed by an unstressed one (DUM dee). Iambs tend to sound lighter and softer, and trochees tend to sound heavier and harder. This is true even in messages as short as brand names. "Feminine" brand names, like Chanel, are often iambs; "masculine" ones, like Black & Decker, tend to be trochees. Most people "feel" this difference even if they find it hard to pinpoint.

Longer messages exploit these metrical differences as well. Traditional English verse forms like iambic pentameter (five iambs per line) go for a softer and more musical quality, as in this line from William Butler Yeats:

When you are old and grey and full of sleep   x / x / x / x / x /

Advertising slogans, like this one from Hallmark, are often based quite directly on verse forms:

WHEN YOU CARE ENOUGH TO SEND THE VERY BEST   x x / x / x / x / x /

Longfellow's poem *The Song of Hiawatha* opts for trochees rather than iambs to produce a strong staccato rhythm that suggests the sound of drums:

On the shores of Gitche Gumee,	/ x / x / x / x
Of the shining Big-Sea-Water,	x x / x / / / x
Stood Nokomis, the old woman,	/ x / x x / / x
Pointing with her finger westward,	/ x / x / x / x

O'er the water pointing westward,	/ x / x / x / x
To the purple clouds of sunset.	/ x / x / x / x

This poem is especially unvarying in its structure—the only notable deviations in this stanza are in the second line and in the phrase "the old woman" in the third line. Then it settles back into very regular trochees. The effect is very noticeable, and very different from the singsongy quality of the earlier Dr. Seuss passage, for example, or the line from Yeats. Poets often vary the rhythms in their poems to avoid monotony. The practice is not that different from the way drummers use fills and other techniques to vary the rhythm in a musical composition. In a micromessage, the danger of having a monotonous rhythm is remote, so the main considerations are to make the rhythm natural and appropriate (or just appropriate, if that means being unnatural).

The old slogan FIFTY-FOUR FORTY OR FIGHT, about an Oregon border dispute, uses a staccato rhythm similar to Longfellow's to create an appropriately aggressive sound. Multiple monosyllabic words with roughly the same degree of emphasis create a rhythm that's very emphatic, like a fist pounding on a table.

LOOSE LIPS SINK SHIPS.

TASTES GREAT, LESS FILLING

Rhythm interacts with other poetic patterns as well, such as *alliteration*, the repetition of consonant sounds in neighboring words. Consider the old Brylcreem slogan, A LITTLE DAB'LL DO YA. A big part of its bounciness comes from the repetition of the "l" sound (and the similar "y" sound) and the "d" sound.

If you want to appreciate rhythm, consider a phrase, like "the rural juror" (which we saw in the last chapter), that utterly lacks it. Poetic language has a lilt to it, a natural music created by the right blend of repetition and contrast. The phrase "rural juror" is a mass of some of the unloveliest syllables of the English language. It has almost none of the contrast between consonants and vowels that usually gives language its shape. And, lacking clear syllable boundaries, it lacks the rhythm of distinct stressed and unstressed syllables.

When you want to give your message music, start where the poets do: with rhythm.

12

PLAY WITH
POETIC PATTERNS

If you think poetry is just for reclusive nineteenth-century ladies and beatniks, you're probably not alone. But keep in mind that poetry is simply a refined expression of the music of language, and that all language is musical. The tools used by poets are also used by songwriters, copywriters, teenagers talking to their friends, and you.

No one knows better than a poet, however, that the sound of a message really matters. The expertise of poets is sometimes tapped by marketers. In the 1950s, the Ford Motor Company unofficially enlisted the help of poet Marianne Moore while trying to name a new car. Moore is familiar to many of us through her widely anthologized poem "Poetry," which begins with the unforgettable line "I, too, dislike it." Moore came up with some pretty unusual names, such as Utopian Turtletop, Mongoose Civique, and Pastelogram. Sadly, the company chose to name the car after Henry Ford's father, Edsel. The Edsel was a failure of legendary proportions. We'll never know how this ill-fated vehicle might have fared if it had been given the bizarre but lovely name Utopian Turtletop.

Poetry is an interesting art, because everyone knows its medium well. It's possible to enjoy visual art and music purely as a consumer. You can go through your entire adult life without producing a single visual image or musical performance. Poetry is different. It's based on a behavior that most of us engage in every day. On the most basic level, we all produce poetry.

It's kind of odd, then, that poetry is often regarded as one of the most rarefied of art forms. Many people simply don't see the poetry in their own language use. They think of language in practical terms—it helps them get things done and, for some, it helps show the world how smart they are. When people relax and get playful with language, they dip their toes into poetry without even knowing it.

Like all other forms of language, poetry is sound and expression, and I'm focusing now on the sound part. What makes a poem special is the way it creates patterns out of sound that can be both lovely and expressive. (Some forms of poetry, such as concrete poetry, use orthography and typography rather than sound, but they're unusual.) One quality that makes things aesthetically pleasing is effortlessness. People like it when they don't have to work too hard. When speaking, effort means having to reconfigure your vocal tract a lot, quickly. When people are learning to speak, or when they're tired, they make slips of the tongue that betray an inability or unwillingness to do that work. The result is *perseveration*, the repetition of a sound or an articulatory gesture where it's not appropriate. Sometimes perseveration affects normal speech. Many people pronounce the word *orangutan* as if it were spelled "orangutang," because it's easier to repeat the "ang" sound than to shift to the front of the mouth to pronounce the phonetically similar "an" sound.

What does that have to do with poetic patterns? Well, people like repetition, and that penchant is partly explained by a desire to avoid extra effort. Poetic language, language that "rolls off the tongue," is filled with repetition. Harmony is the sunny side of laziness.

The most obvious type of repetition is rhyme, in which the final emphasized syllable of a word or phrase, and everything following it, is repeated. Rhyme is used in micromessages ranging from company names like JotSpot to Johnny Cochran's famous defense slogan from the 1995 O. J. Simpson murder trial: IF IT DOES NOT FIT, YOU MUST ACQUIT.

Rhyme is all over the place: children's books, colloquial sayings, nursery rhymes, song lyrics, slogans, and of course, poetry. We really notice rhyming words when they occur at the ends of separate lines or phrases of the same length, as in the most overt forms of rhyming poetry, such as the limerick. The slogan OH THANK HEAVEN FOR 7-ELEVEN fits that pattern. Rhymes can also occur inside lines and phrases, the way "7" and "Eleven" do in this slogan. So-called internal rhyme is a common feature in rap, because it accentuates the quick, complex rhythms that rappers favor. Here's a little snippet from Rakim:

> *It's biting me, fighting me, inviting me to rhyme*
> —*Rakim, from "Erik B. Is President"*

The prevalence of this kind of internal rhyme in rap prompted Tom Robbins to make the following observation in his novel *Skinny Legs and All*:

> *Rap music . . . sounds like somebody feeding a rhyming dictionary to a popcorn popper.*

But internal rhyme is not unique to poetry and rap. Here it is in a six-word memoir:

Conceived, implored, employed, adored, retired, ignored.
—Joy MacKenzie, quoted on the BBC Today *website*

And here are just some of the many slogans that use it:

EVERYTHING'S BETTER WITH BLUE BONNET ON IT

THE INCREDIBLE EDIBLE EGG

ACE IS THE PLACE WITH THE HELPFUL HARDWARE MAN

SOOTHING INFECTION PROTECTION

BOUNTY, IT'S THE QUICKER PICKER-UPPER

FILL IT TO THE RIM WITH BRIM

MUST-SEE TV *(NBC)*

Rhymes create implicit comparisons between words. While 7-Eleven's slogan doesn't explicitly claim that its stores are like heaven—it simply uses the word *heaven* in a common phrase of exclamation—the fact that both words in the name 7-Eleven rhyme with *heaven* implies that claim subtly.

Besides perfect rhymes, there are near-rhymes that shade into *assonance*, the repetition of vowel sounds. We find assonance in movie titles such as *Five Easy Pieces* and *The French Connection*. The United Airlines slogan FLY THE FRIENDLY SKIES has a near-rhyme between the first and last words that creates an appealing symmetry. The GE slogan WE BRING GOOD THINGS TO LIFE gets a musical quality from the near-rhyme between *bring* and *things*. The Paul Masson wine slogan WE WILL SELL NO WINE BEFORE ITS TIME is memorable largely for the near-rhyme between *wine* and *time*. Democratic vice presidential candidate Joe Biden used near-rhyme when he made this comment about John McCain during the 2008 election: "You can't call yourself a maverick when all you've ever been is a sidekick." Here's a near-rhyming bumper sticker: KEEP YOUR ROSARIES OUT OF MY OVARIES. Even more subtle repetition of vowel sounds can add music to small messages such as INTEL INSIDE; FRESH MEX (Chevys); DON'T LEAVE HOME WITHOUT IT (American Express); and SOUP IS GOOD FOOD (Campbell Soup).

The sounds that participate in poetic patterning usually occur in syllables that are emphasized and words that have important meanings. The best examples use words that sound natural and that just happen to create a pattern. When word choice is driven by the desire to create a rhyme or other pattern, the result can be clunky and corny sounding. For example, One Hour Heating & Air Conditioning uses the slogan ALWAYS ON TIME . . . OR YOU DON'T PAY A DIME, which requires the cliché "don't pay a dime" in order to rhyme.

Most poems are meant to be spoken, and their patterns are temporal and rhythmic, like musical patterns. Let's consider the beginning of another famous poem by the Irish poet William Butler Yeats:

> *I will arise and go now, and go to Innisfree,*
> *And a small cabin build there, of clay and wattles made:*
> *Nine bean-rows will I have there, a hive for the honey-bee;*
> *And live alone in the bee-loud glade.*

This stanza has a very songlike quality, and like music, it's patterned at different levels. The whole poem has three stanzas, each containing four lines. The first three lines of each stanza are similar in length, and the last line is shorter. The end of the first line rhymes with the end of the third, and the end of the second rhymes with the end of the fourth. This is what we might call the macrostructure of the poem, and it's mostly not relevant to microstyle. But now let's consider the microstructure, the structure we find inside of each line. There's a noticeable pattern in the first three lines that goes something like this:

BEAT BEAT BEAT *(pause)* BEAT BEAT BEAT *(pause)*

The beats are made by the emphasized syllables in the line. The pauses are made by natural breaks in the syntax. Now let's take a close look at the last two lines:

Nine bean-rows will I have there, a hive for the honey-bee;
And live alone in the bee-loud glade.

Notice the repetition of the "n" and "h" sounds in the first line. Also notice that the "b" sound occurs near the beginning and end of the line. Finally, and most dramatically, the "l" sound makes four appearances in the second line. The repetition of consonants is perhaps the most important and noticeable poetic device after rhyme. When the consonants occur at the beginnings of words or stressed syllables, we call it *alliteration*. When they occur all over the place, like the "n" sounds in "nine bean rows," we call it *consonance* (though sometimes *alliteration* is used as a blanket term). One famous English poet who really squeezed everything he could out of alliteration was Gerard Manley Hopkins. He wrote many lines like the following (repeated consonant sounds appear below the line):

As kingfishers catch fire, dragonflies draw flame.
K   f   r k   f r dr   fl   dr   fl

Like rhyme, alliteration calls attention to the words or syllables in which it occurs. Marianne Moore's Utopian Turtletop is notable for the way it repeats the "t" sound. Alliteration brings poetry to real brand names as well, from Dunkin' Donuts to Coca-Cola to Google. And alliteration and consonance occur in slogans:

BETTER BUILT, BETTER BACKED *(Mitsubishi)*

BAYER WORKS WONDERS

FLY THE FRIENDLY SKIES *(United Airlines)*

RELAX, IT'S FEDEX

LEAVE THE DRIVING TO US *(Greyhound)*

REACH OUT AND TOUCH SOMEONE *(AT&T)*

MILK. IT DOES A BODY GOOD. *(National Dairy Board)*

TIPPECANOE AND TYLER, TOO! *(William Henry Harrison's 1840 campaign slogan)*

Alliteration is also used in corporate mantras, such as Nike's AUTHENTIC ATHLETIC PERFORMANCE and Target's DEMOCRATIZE DESIGN. Alliteration is everywhere. It's in common expressions such as *road rage, french fries,* and *fashion faux-pas.* It's in movie titles such as *Dawn of the Dead, Desperately Seeking Susan, King Kong, Leaving Las Vegas, Double Indemnity, Close Encounters of the Third Kind, Mad Max, The Way We Were, The Seven Samurai, Married to the Mob, McCabe and Mrs. Miller,* and countless others. It's in book titles both classic (*Pride and Prejudice*; *Sense and Sensibility*; *Of Mice and Men*) and recent (*Good to Great*; *The One Minute Millionaire*; *The Mind of the Market*; *Jesus, Jobs, and Justice*; *Moral Minds*; *Wired for War*; *The Power of Pull*). It's in TV show titles such as *Mad Men* and *Golden Girls.* It's in tweets:

> *The 1950s seem like they were just hamburgers, haircuts, and hatred.*
>
> *— @TheSulk (Alec Sulkin), April 12, 2010*

and it's in six-word memoirs:

Pickles, pregnancy, puking, pain, premature. Priceless.
—*Sherry Rentschler, quoted in* It All Changed
in an Instant: More Six-Word Memoirs

Poetry is all around us. Add a little to your micromessages and make them sing.

13

MAKE THE SOUND FIT

Sometimes sounds fit very specific meanings, as in onomatopoetic words—that is, words that sound like what they mean—such as *buzz*, *whoosh*, and *smack*. This kind of relation between sound and meaning is a sort of resemblance or iconicity. The perceived resemblance between speech sounds and nonspeech sounds is only the most obvious kind of iconicity, which can be quite abstract. In the I LIKE IKE example, the relationships between syllables iconically represent a spatial arrangement that serves as a metaphor for the emotional relationships between Eisenhower and his supporters. Complicated, but effective—and it just sounds good.

Iconicity can also be based more on the way it feels to say sounds than on what it's like to hear them. Try saying the name Mounds, for the Hershey's candy bar. You might notice that your mouth pantomimes taking a bite of something: your lips part, reach out and pull back in, and your front teeth start to come together.

It might seem that the range of things that sounds can represent iconically would be fairly limited. However, people regularly associate sounds with the physical properties of objects. This is called *sound symbolism*, and it greatly expands the expressive power of consonants and vowels. Consider this simple example that we used at Lexicon Branding: match the made-up words *taketa* and *naluma* with the following two drawings:

Without hesitation, you almost certainly matched *taketa* with the angular drawing and *naluma* with the curved one. This particular contrast is based mostly on *sonority*, the extent to which a spoken sound involves an uninterrupted flow of air and vibration of the vocal folds. We perceive sounds with high sonority (that is, with a lack of obstruction or interruption in their pronunciation) as softer and rounder than sounds with low sonority, and those tangible properties in turn suggest a number of more abstract ones: gentle, "feminine," etc. Brand names regularly make use of the symbolic properties of sonority. Consider the strong tendency for beauty products to have high-sonority brand names: Chanel, L'Oréal, Revlon, Avon, etc. For the sake of contrast, consider brand names for power tools, which tend to have lower-sonority sounds: Black & Decker, Craftsman, Ridgid, etc.

Vowels, too, can suggest physical properties. Consider the nonsense words *geep* and *gop*, and match them up with the circles shown here:

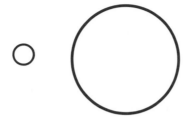

You probably matched *geep* with the small circle, and *gop* with the large one. Experts disagree on exactly why people have these associations. It may have to do with prominent frequencies in the sounds. The vowel in *geep* sounds higher than the vowel in *gop*, and for acoustic reasons we expect high sounds to come from small things. On the other hand, when we pronounce the vowel in *geep*, we make a very small space between the tongue and palate, so it might be more a matter of how it feels to say the word. Whatever the reason, people consistently make the same judgments about the relative sizes of these two sounds.

Sonority isn't the only basis for sound symbolism. Other properties of sounds can also suggest meanings. For example, alveolar sounds like the ones represented by the letters *t, d, s, l, r,* and *n,* which are produced lightly with the tongue behind the top front teeth, tend to suggest smallness and lightness. Consider how well the expressions *itty-bitty* and *eensy-weensy* fit their meanings, and how strange it would seem to use the expression *oomby-boomby* for the same meaning. In the book *Ounce Dice Trice*, poet Alastair Reid proposes appropriate proper names for different kinds of things. For insects, he suggests the names Twilliter, Limlet, Tilltin, Legliddy, and Tristram—notice the preponderance of alveolar sounds in these names for tiny creatures.

Names can use specific sounds to support their meanings. The name Etsy, for an online marketplace dealing in handmade goods, sounds very small, both through its allusion to the expression *itsy-bitsy* and through the same alveolar sounds that occur in Reid's insect names. The concept of smallness fits the company; it conveys the idea that the merchandise on the site is made in small quantities on a small scale (usually by individuals rather than companies), and Etsy itself is a small company. Also, smallness suggests precision and attention to minute detail, which is perfect for handmade goods.

Sometimes sound symbolism works directly against intended meaning. Consider the file synchronization software called Syncplicity. Its main function is to combine files from different computers effortlessly. Think about that, and think about the name, which combines two words. They had an opportunity here to represent the software's function iconically with a seamless, flowing blend of words. Needless to say, they didn't achieve that. The horrible knot of consonants between the first two syllables makes Syncplicity about as far from seamless and flowing as a word blend can get without being unpronounceable.

Sound symbolism is a mysterious tool that relies on the intrinsic properties of speech sounds, bypassing the social conventions that connect words and their meanings. It can add an ineffable richness to a miniature message.

STRUCTURE

Grammar gives language its expressive power, allowing us to combine familiar units to express novel ideas. We can say just about everything we want to say with language, and that adaptability comes from its multitiered organization. At the lowest level are individual speech sounds. English uses just twenty-four consonants and fewer vowels as building blocks for tens of thousands of words and an uncountable number of possible sentences. Apart from sound symbolism, discussed in Chapter 13, the individual sounds don't have meanings. They exist simply to be distinguished from one another and put together to create units that *can* express meaning.

Then comes the real engine of expressive creativity. It consists of *morphology* (rules for creating complex words) and *syntax* (rules for creating sentences). Linguists sometimes lump these together using the term *morphosyntax*, because they're closely related. In some languages, most sentences are like long words, so morphology and syntax are essentially the same thing. In languages like English, syntax does most of the heavy lifting in sentence construction, but morphology is still closely related because it expresses grammatical agreement and other information that depends on syntactic context.

In English, we use morphological patterns when we create new words. Using them well means creating words that make sense, seem structurally natural, and have a smooth sound.

The syntactic patterns of English are more numerous and complex. True language geeks like to play with them. Poets such as E. E. Cummings push the expressive power of language by bending and breaking the rules of syntax. Consider the first two lines of his poem "anyone lived in a pretty how town":

> *anyone lived in a pretty how town*
> *with up so floating many bells down*

Cummings surprises the reader by putting words where they don't belong, syntactically speaking. For example, in the first line the question word *how* appears where we might expect an adjective. The second line seems to be the phrase "with so many bells," but interrupted in odd places by the words *up* and *floating*, and with the word *down* stuck on at the end. The rest of the poem is filled with similar deviations from normal syntax. The overall effect is disorienting, and that helps give Cummings's poems a magical quality.

Linguists also like to play with syntax. My dissertation adviser, Charles Fillmore, invents and collects absurd sentences that illustrate different grammatical phenomena. One day in syntax class he was talking about preposition stranding—ending a sentence with a preposition that isn't followed by its object, because the object appears earlier in the sentence. Many prescriptivists object to preposition stranding, while descriptivists observe that it's perfectly natural and has been part of English for a long time. Winston Churchill, of all people, is often credited, probably falsely, with the quote, "Ending a sentence with a preposition is something up with which I will not put," illustrating the absurdities that can result from following the rule to the letter. In trying to think of how many prepositions could accumulate at the end of a sentence, Fillmore came up with the following:

What did you bring that book that I didn't want to be read to out of about Down Under up for?

This sentence ends with seven prepositions: "out of about Down Under up for." Okay, not really, because *Down Under*, a nickname for Australia, is really one proper noun rather than two prepositions. But it's a great sentence anyway. If you're a language geek, that is.

Some people get the impression that syntax is like math with words instead of numbers, and it's not hard to see why. Noam Chomsky, the most influential linguist of the second half of the twentieth century, made his name with a theory of syntax that was all about formal symbol manipulation. He sought to model people's subconscious knowledge about sentence structure using abstract grammatical symbols and formal rules for manipulating them, similar to the ones being developed by computer scientists at the time. Such rule systems are in fact considered to be a part of applied mathematics. In the earliest versions of Chomsky's theory, presented in the book *Syntactic Structures* and other works, he described syntactic patterns using symbols for abstract word and phrase categories (such as noun, noun phrase, verb, verb phrase) with no reference to the meanings of the words involved. Syntactic rules consisted of formal operations that would take these symbols as inputs and "generate" structures from them in a consistent, rote way—the way a computer might do it. For that reason, Chomsky's theory became known as "generative grammar."

The purpose of a grammar for Chomsky was to represent the

knowledge that a person needs to speak a language, producing all the possible grammatical sentences and no ungrammatical ones, and that purpose remains the goal for most linguists to this day.

I know what you're thinking: "But people produce ungrammatical sentences all the time!" There are two answers to that. First, the kind of grammaticality you have in mind isn't a linguist's grammaticality. And second, even linguists recognize that people make mistakes sometimes. If they're able to recognize a mistake as a mistake, then they still have the knowledge that linguists try to describe. And if they don't recognize a mistake as a mistake, then it's not a mistake. I know that seems sort of circular, but it makes sense if you're being descriptive rather than prescriptive. Just think about it for a while.

But back to the main point. Chomsky used the following now famous example to show that a sentence can be grammatical without making any logical sense:

Colorless green ideas sleep furiously.

This example provided a rationale for isolating syntactic structure from meaning, and allowing syntax to really focus just on the former. The history of syntax since Chomsky, however, has featured the gradual reintroduction of the missing element of meaning. An early criticism of Chomsky's theory, for example, maintained that it's the job of a syntactic theory to account for the fact that transitive verbs occur in sentences with direct objects, as in "They ate their sandwiches," and intransitive verbs occur in sentences without, as in "They slept well." The distinction between transitive and intransitive is largely a matter of meaning, because it has to do with the number of participants and props involved in the situation represented by a verb. Eating involves two, for example (an eater and something that gets eaten), while sleeping involves just one (the sleeper). All current syntactic theories include a way to match verbs with syntactic contexts that fit their meanings in this respect.

Another problem for meaningless syntax was the existence of idioms such as "kick the bucket." In Chomsky's theory, words expressed meanings, but syntactic rules combined words with no regard for their meanings. This model implied that to understand a whole sentence, you just needed to know the meanings of the words it contained and how they were put together syntactically. What makes an idiom special is that its meaning can't be figured out that way. Kicking the bucket has nothing to do with kicking or with buckets. To correctly use an idiom, a person has to learn a whole phrase or sentence pattern and associate it with a meaning. In Chomsky's theory there was no way to represent such a pairing between complex grammatical form and meaning.

"Kick the bucket" is sort of the prototypical idiom. It always includes the same words and is just flexible enough, grammatically speaking, to allow suffixes on the verb *kick*. If idioms were no more than that, they probably wouldn't have posed much of a challenge for a syntactic theory. The *mental lexicon* (the storehouse of words we have in our memories) could surely accommodate such expressions fairly simply; they would be essentially multiword words.

But idioms go beyond expressions like "kick the bucket." What really defines an idiom is the fact that it's a whole phrase or sentence pattern that has to be memorized and associated with a meaning. Many idioms are like phrase or clause templates with few or even no specific words filled in. One example is the pattern of sentences like "The more you eat, the more you want" and "The bigger they are, the harder they fall." Expressions that fit this pattern don't even conform to the normal rules of grammar. Most sentences have a main verb that organizes the meaning of the whole sentence, but neither of these sample sentences has a main verb.

They both consist of two odd comparative noun phrases. Because expressions like these depart from syntactic rules that are in effect in all the rest of the grammar, those syntactic rules certainly can't provide the basis for figuring out their meaning.

Some people call expressions like these "semi-idiomatic constructions" or "constructional idioms." Others use the less descriptive but more playful term "snowclones."

Why do we have idioms? One possible answer is that once people begin to create a particular phrase or sentence pattern with regularity, it can take on a life of its own, and the search for relevance can lead it to acquire its own "portable context" and meaning.

All this talk about idioms and snowclones is pretty abstract without a concrete example. So let's take a look at a particular constructional idiom, along with some evidence and speculation about how it might have come into existence. Here's an example:

THERE'S ONLY SO SLOWLY YOU CAN DRIVE ON THE
FREEWAY.

You've probably heard sentences like this. If you think they're grammatically peculiar, you're right. The especially strange thing about this sentence is the beginning: "There's only so . . ." That would actually be a normal way to begin a sentence like this:

THERE'S ONLY SO MUCH YOU CAN DO TO HELP AT
THIS POINT.

This more normal sentence is what grammarians call an existential statement, along the lines of "There are penguins in Antarctica," but a little more complex. Existential sentences follow a pretty strict pattern. Like our strange sentence, in their basic form they have the word *there* followed by some form of the linking verb *be*. What comes after that, however, other than an adverb or two, is a noun phrase. This is such a strong generalization that grammatical theories usually specify some sort of special relation between this use of the word *there* and noun phrases.

Our weird sentence, "There's only so slowly you can drive on the freeway," doesn't have that noun phrase after the verb *be*. Instead it has a special kind of relative clause in which an adverb phrase or adjective phrase (in this case the adverb phrase "so slowly") has been put in front. That's no normal existential sentence. Our weird sentence, and other sentences that follow the same pattern, include the word *can* or *could* inside the relative clause. In fact, corresponding to sentences that fit the strange pattern are paraphrases that don't look like existential sentences, but that also have one of these words:

You can only drive so slowly on the freeway.

We could only drive so fast in the snow.

Strange patterns like the one we see in "There's only so slowly you can drive on the freeway" go through steps in their historical development. It's like one of those puzzles in which you have to turn one word into another word by changing only one letter at a time, with each change resulting in a word. Let's consider the stages that this construction might have gone through. A pivotal phrase seems to be "so much," since it connects the dots between existential statements with the expected noun phrases, and existential statements without. In some cases "so much" is used literally for a quantity of a measurable substance:

There's only so much clean water to go around.

There's only so much hard labor one person
can do.

In other cases the noun is omitted because it's understood in context:

THERE'S ONLY SO MUCH TO GO AROUND.

THERE'S ONLY SO MUCH ONE PERSON CAN DO.

Presto! That gets us started with the pattern "so _____ ," where the blank is filled in with a word that represents a scale of quantity. Besides the noun quantifier *much* occurring without a noun phrase, there are also sentences in which words such as *far* (for a scale of distance) and *long* (for a scale of time) are used instead:

THERE'S ONLY SO FAR A PERSON CAN GO.

THERE'S ONLY SO LONG A PERSON CAN WAIT.

That pattern seems to have been extended gradually over historical time to include different kinds of scale words. An online search of ProQuest Historical Newspapers turned up the following. First there were uses of the pattern with *much* plus a noun phrase:

There is only so much volume of currency. (1899)
There is only so much of the metal in the ground. (1915)
There is only so much work to be done. (1945)

In 1956 there appeared examples without the noun phrase:

There is only so much and no more that writers can do with one person and still keep him interesting and amusing.

In 1973, the pattern appeared with *far* rather than *much*:

There is only so far business will go without a law with teeth.

In 1981, the pattern was first used with *long*:

There is only so long that they can stay under water. (said of companies selling US dollars while their value increases)

Other types of adjectives and adverbs are tough to find in newspapers, probably because they sound informal and slangy, but you can find them all over the web. Try it yourself. Just do the following search on Google:

"THERE'S ONLY SO" -"THERE'S ONLY SO MUCH"
-"THERE'S ONLY SO MANY"

This search finds the pattern "there's only so" and eliminates the most frequent results, in which *so* is followed by *much* or *many*. Then you'll see examples like this:

There's only so often you can talk or sneak your way out of a fight.
There's only so fast you can dance.
There's only so long fake thugs can pretend.
    (attributed to rapper Jay-Z)

Doing an exercise like this shows you how the official grammar you find in textbooks and style guides morphs into the living grammar you see on the web and hear in conversation.

Chapters 14–20 look at different ways that morphological and syntactic structure are used in microstyle.

14

BREAK THE RULES

As I discussed in the Introduction, Big Style encouraged us to focus more on correct form in our writing than on message. While that may have brought a pleasing predictability and elegance to what we wrote, it also took a lot of the fun out of writing. It probably doesn't need to be said at this point, but when you're using microstyle, it's not always necessary to follow the rules of grammar and spelling. Rule breaking can be expressive. E. E. Cummings did it, after all. Good microstyle doesn't require rule breaking, but it does require a playful attitude. Give yourself permission not to care so much about being correct. Focus on what works and what sounds good to you. And when you have a good reason, go ahead and break the rules.

But remember, I'm giving you a linguist's perspective on this issue, and linguists tend toward a descriptive rather than a prescriptive view of language. Being descriptive means trying to understand what forms people actually use and why. But there's a complication here: linguists are also people, and when we're simply being people we have preferences about language just like everyone else. It's what we conclude from these preferences that's different. We don't assume that people with different preferences are destroying the language and must be stopped. I like what Mark Liberman, a linguist who writes for the Language Log blog, had to say about this. He rejects the "descriptivist" label, and opts instead for the "rational people" label: "We don't worship our own prejudices, and we're more curious than censorious."

SPELLING

Misspellings are used as much for practical reasons as for expressive ones. In trademark law, misspelling a real word can make it easier to register and protect as a trademark. Consumer products have given us countless strategic misspellings, such as Cheez Whiz, Rice Krispies, Handi Wipes, and Reddi-wip. In the world of domain names, almost all the correctly spelled single-word ".com" domains have already been registered. So if you want to leverage the pithy meaning of a single word, you either have to spend thousands of dollars to buy a registered domain from its owner, or you have to get creative with your spelling. That's why misspellings have been such a big part of the Web 2.0 landscape, with names like Tumblr (for a sort of mini blogging service) and Google (based on *googol*, a word for a very large number). Misspellings like that also make names more distinctive for search engines.

Spelling can be used creatively in other ways. Clay Shirky, the NYU professor, author, and social media commentator, used the following bio on his Twitter profile:

Bald. Unreliable. Easily distracte

The unfinished last word in his bio is funny; it illustrates the last of the unflattering qualities he attributes to himself. This example also belongs in Chapter 9 ("Say the Wrong Thing") because there's a strong expectation that a Twitter bio will highlight something appealing about a Twitter user. Of course, Shirky's bio does highlight something appealing about him—his sense of humor—but to discover that message we have to take a step beyond the message that he pretends to give us. The unfinished message is a bit of a trope on Twitter—perhaps not surprisingly, since the most challenging aspect of using the service is the 140-character limit. Here's another example:

> *The three worst mistakes you can make are overpromising and underdelivering.*
> — *@Dwineman, quoted in* Twitter Wit

The unfinished message trope calls attention to the act of creating a message. Shirky's Twitter bio suggests that he actually got distracted while typing it. The tweet from Dwineman let's us catch him in the act of underdelivering. This is an interesting and unusual way to evoke a specific, concrete situation (see Chapter 5).

GRAMMAR

Grammar is a battlefield. It's not standardized the way spelling is, though people have certainly tried. Where grammar is concerned, it's often hard to determine whether "rules" have been broken. Consider the controversial Apple slogan:

THINK DIFFERENT

Apple took a lot of heat in the 1990s when it unveiled this slogan. Self-appointed language bosses declared that the slogan should be "think differently." Why did Apple go with THINK DIFFER-ENT? First, it seems likely that the slogan alludes to, or at least is inspired by, the THINK SMALL campaign for the Volkswagen Beetle that we encountered in Chapter 9. *Small*, like *different*, is an adjective rather than an adverb, and could be considered incorrect in the Volkswagen slogan.

Under the surface of grammatical disputes like this, however, there's usually some hidden complexity that makes the "incorrect" form less incorrect than it seems. There are, in fact, perfectly correct uses of adjectives that look like the uses in these slogans. First there's the depictive adjective—one that describes the state of one of the participants or props in an action. For example, you can "eat carrots raw" or "eat carrots naked." *Raw* characterizes the state of the carrots when they're eaten, and *naked* describes the state of the eater. Because the adjectives clearly do not modify the verb here, this is a clear case: no one would say "eat carrots rawly" or "eat carrots nakedly." Another example is "the engine runs a little hot"; here *hot* is an adjective that describes the state of the engine when it's running.

What about the question "How do you feel?" When we use *feel* to refer to emotions or general well-being rather than touching things with our hands, it's followed by an adjective that names a general emotional or physical state: "I feel good," "I feel bad," "I feel sick," and so on. In these cases the adjectives don't modify the word *feel*, but complement or complete it. *Feel* needs that adjective—you can't just answer "I feel" to this question. These are all perfectly correct uses of adjectives, yet you'll come across people saying, "I feel badly about that," because they've been taught to use adverbs to modify verbs and think this is a case of verb modification.

With the verb *think*, things get trickier still. Sometimes *think* takes adverbs, plain and simple; you can "think clearly," for example. Other times *think* occurs with a word or phrase that characterizes the content of the thoughts in question. The kinds of phrases that can play the role are varied: you can "think great thoughts" (noun phrase), or "think that you're a rock star" (complement clause), or "think about quitting your job" (prepositional phrase). An idiomatic use of *think* followed by a single noun or adjective that names the subject of one's thoughts fits this pattern: "think small" and "think different."

Subway's slogan, EAT FRESH, complicates matters even more. The verb *eat*, unlike the verb *think*, is a straightforward transitive verb that typically takes a noun phrase object, as in "I ate a sandwich." In this slogan it occurs with an adjective, *fresh*. To make sense of Subway's slogan, we have to recognize that there's a broader pattern of using adjectives as adverbs in certain contexts. People say things like "living cheap," "driving slow," and "eating healthy" all the time, even though such phrases may be considered incorrect. Subway's slogan fits into that vernacular pattern.

Another unusual use of adjectives occurs in HP's slogan, LET's DO AMAZING. This is an example of another idiom, or special construction. We also see it in the title of the Tyler Perry movie *I Can Do Bad All by Myself.* The idiom is often used in the negative. For example, someone might say "I don't *do* nice," with an appropriately vicious inflection.

Sometimes a genuine grammatical violation acknowledged even by descriptivists might be committed in the name of word-play. Betty Crocker used the slogan BAKE SOMEONE HAPPY, which puts the word *bake* in a syntactic context where it doesn't belong. Instead, that context belongs to the word *make*.

There are other expressive ways to violate grammar. You might say, "This failed" or "This was a failure," but a more recent usage, popularized by FailBlog, is simply to use the form *fail* as an interjection, as in "Fail!"; or to use it as a noun, as in "It's a big fail." This new usage is probably inspired in part by the use of "pass" and "fail" as grades in school. *Pass* and *fail* would usually be used as verbs, but in the context of grades they become nouns, like other grades: "I got a pass/fail/B+ on my paper." Somehow this usage has a certain oomph that's lacking in the verb form and in the noun *failure*. It evokes a faceless authority passing judgment, and summons up an image of a big rubber stamp coming down on a test or a report.

So, go forth and break rules, if it sounds right. And if you don't mind the Grammar Police getting on your back.

15

COIN A NEW WORD

In 2007, at PodCamp Pittsburgh 2, a social media "unconference," some geeks were sitting around discussing web technology—and going off on tangents. According to Andy Quayle, one of the participants, "We were talking about different meats and international types of bacon and were receiving messages on our mobile devices and eventually the two mixed." A new word was born: *bacn*, which the group defined as 'email you want—but not right now.' *Bacn* refers to the email we sign up to receive—notifications from Facebook, beta announcements from startups, etc.—and never get around to reading. Bacn is spam's tastier cousin.

Being geeks, these neologists—that is, creators of *neologisms*, or new words—made a website to promote their word and asked bloggers to write about it. Their promotional efforts paid off. *Bacn* became a story. Not everyone liked the new word. Some commenters on the Bacn website pointed out that bacon, the food, is simply too delicious to serve as a good metaphor for email you never get around to reading. But the story of Bacn spread. It was covered by CNET, *InformationWeek*, *New Scientist* magazine, National Public Radio, *Wired* magazine, and even *People* magazine.

Bacn was coined to attract attention, communicate instantly, and be remembered and repeated. It worked. Notice the big story wasn't that people sign up to receive email and then don't read it. The story was that someone had come up with a funny, catchy *name* for the common phenomenon that makes us see it in an interesting light. Neologisms can be among the most powerful of micromessages.

Coined words come in many varieties. There are political epithets like *Defeatocrat*; terms for new technologies and cultural phenomena like *podcast, greenwash*, and of course *bacn*; proprietary names for companies and products, such as *Skype, Technorati, Wii*, and more.

Almost all new words, from tech company names to political insults, result from a handful of processes familiar to linguists. Most of these processes are green: they reuse or recycle existing words. Here are seven common ways to build a new word:

1. Reuse an existing word (*Apple, spam*)
2. Create a new compound word by sticking two words together (*YouTube, website*)
3. Create a blend by combining part of a word with another word or word part (*Technorati, Defeatocrat*)
4. Attach a prefix or a suffix to a word (*Uncola, Feedster*)
5. Make something up out of arbitrary syllables (*Bebo*)
6. Make an analogy or play on words (*Farecast, podcast*)
7. Create an acronym (*GUBA, scuba*)

Making up a new word doesn't have to mean creating a new sound; it can also mean putting an existing sound to new use.

People often don't think of these as neologisms, but the end result is essentially a new word. Remember, a word isn't just a sound or a handful of letters; what makes it interesting, what makes it a *word*, is that it has a meaning. When people use the word *word*, they sort of vacillate between meaning just the spoken and written form on the one hand, and the form plus the meaning on the other. For this reason, lexical semanticists—linguists who really take words seriously—don't even find the word *word* very useful. They use different terms when they're talking about the form alone and when they're talking about the form plus its meaning.

To put a special mark of ownership on a repurposed word, you can respell it. Respelling words serves some technical functions: as we saw in the last chapter, it makes them easier to trademark (as in Rice Krispies, Cheez Whiz, and Krazy Glue), it often creates a unique keyword to increase search engine visibility (as in Squidoo), and it sometimes makes it possible to acquire a meaningful ".com" domain (as in Topix, a localized news service). But respelling comes at a cost: you run the risk of seeming stupid or cheesy, or being confusing.

One of the best respelling techniques eliminates letters that aren't necessary for pronunciation. This approach achieves spelling economy, a desirable quality in a name. Flickr, for example, eliminates the *e* in the common *-er* ending. Eliminating letters that are not pronounced is a natural move, and one that children often do. At the end of his kindergarten year, my son Tobias unwittingly coined a Web 2.0 name when he described himself in a written report as "organisd."

Reusing a word—that is, giving it a new meaning—can change it forever in people's minds. *Spam*, once a brand name for a humble canned meat product, provides a perfect example. Recycling words—recombining them into new, larger units, sometimes breaking them down into their component pieces first—offers almost limitless possibilities for new coinages.

Coining words is an English literary tradition. William Shakespeare was an avid neologist. Some words that we still use today, and many others that we don't, made their first appearance in one of his plays. Shakespeare's interest in new words was poetic rather than informational, however; he strove less to name new ideas than to express old ones so that they fit the cadences of his characters' voices. The poetic use of neologism goes back even further in the history of our language. Old English epic poems such as *Beowulf* contained numerous *kennings*, fanciful compounds that replaced simple nouns with sometimes riddlelike descriptions. For example, a ship might be described as a "sea-steed," or blood as "slaughter-dew."

Words coined for special occasions without any concern for their permanence are called *nonce* words. Perhaps one of the best known coiners of English nonce words is Lewis Carroll. Many people have encountered his nonsensical poem "Jabberwocky," which appears in the book *Through the Looking Glass* and is filled with words of Carroll's invention:

> *Twas brillig, and the slithy toves*
> *Did gyre and gimble in the wabe*
> *All mimsy were the borogoves*
> *And the mome raths outgrabe.*

Humpty Dumpty later explains to Alice the meaning of part of this poem:

> *Well, "slithy" means "lithe and slimy." "Lithe" is the same as "active." You see it's like a portmanteau—there are two meanings packed into one word.*

He also explains that *mimsy* is a blend of *miserable* and *flimsy*.

We now have other, less literary reasons to create new words.

They help us keep pace with the rapid rate of change in science, technology, business, and society. Neologism is such a salient feature of tech-obsessed American culture that there's a feature in *Wired* magazine devoted to it. The web makes tracking new words much easier than it was in the past. Several websites, such as Word Spy, are devoted solely to spotting and documenting neologisms.

Good neologisms sound fresh and perfectly natural at the same time. Naturalness results from respecting the normal cadences of speech and the sounds of the words used, as well as the meanings and grammatical functions of the component parts. Biznik, the name of a social network for independent businesspeople, is a perfect use of the Yiddish-derived suffix *-nik*, which attaches to nouns and describes people who have an affinity for what the noun names (*beatnik, peacenik*).

It's surprising how many new words are poorly constructed. The old IBM computer name Aptiva sounds odd if you think of it as consisting of the word *apt* and the suffix *-ive* with a Latinate vowel at the end. The *-ive* suffix attaches to verbs to make adjectives (*creative* from *create, divisive* from *divide*, etc.), but *apt* is already an adjective, so Aptiva just seems a little off.

Neologism is the ultimate in microstyle, because it involves poking around under the hood of words and tinkering with their internal structure. Even if you just stick two words together to make a compound, as in YouTube, you create a word-internal syllable boundary, which can be a sticking point in pronunciation. But what really calls for some finesse with verbal mechanics is the blend word, or *portmanteau*.

In a well-constructed portmanteau, two component words blend together seamlessly through a phonetic overlap or similarity. Consider the word *vegangelical*, a blend of *evangelical* and *vegan*. While *vegan* doesn't rhyme with the first two syllables of *evangelical*, it does have the same vowel sounds (when *evangelical* has a fully unemphasized and neutral second vowel). There's also a shared "v" sound, even though it occurs in a slightly different place. The result of combining these words is apt, both semantically and phonologically. Another interesting blend is *adhocracy*, a combination of *ad hoc* and *democracy*.

Bad blends try to squish words together in unnatural ways. Foodportunity, a networking event for food journalists, got its terrible name when someone stuck the whole word *food* into a spot previously occupied by a syllable consisting of only a single vowel. The huge phonetic difference between these two parts makes the neologism sound unnatural. Other bad blends fail to preserve the patterns of syllable emphasis of their component words. I like to call this phenomenon *awkwordplay*, a blend of *awkward* and *wordplay*, because that name actually demonstrates the phenomenon. If you try to pronounce the word *awkward* correctly, with no emphasis on the second syllable, then *wordplay* sounds all wrong. If you pronounce *wordplay* correctly, with emphasis on the first syllable, *awkward* gets all messed up. There's no nice, natural way to pronounce this word. A real example of awkwordplay is the name Teensurance, for a teen insurance policy from Safeco. The one-syllable word *teen* requires its own emphasis, but it replaces the unemphasized first syllable of *insurance*, resulting in a clunky name.

Perhaps the easiest way to create a new word is to simply stick two existing words together to make a compound. Political appellations that use this pattern include *wingnuts* (extreme right-wingers), *moonbats* (extreme lefties), and *Islamofascists* (which uses the classical compound-forming *o* to connect its two parts).

THE WORD FACTORY

Ludwig Wittgenstein, the philosopher we met in Chapter 8, compared the lexicon of a language to an old city. The grammatical words—auxiliary verbs, prepositions, and such—he likened to the ancient city center. There you find odd nooks and crannies that have been preserved for centuries. The vocabularies of mathematics and other technical fields he compared to orderly new subdivisions. To extend the analogy in an obvious way, brand names, URLs, and other such purpose-driven neologisms are the storefronts in the bustling commercial strips and shopping malls of the language. New ones pop up all the time, and a few succeed and become enduring parts of the landscape.

Brand names, in particular, are an interesting species. Unlike most other neologisms, they sometimes seem to be made out of whole cloth: Nerf, Kodak, Oreo. They're highly artificial, designed with great care for commercial purposes, but they're bona fide words of our language. Some even make the transition from proper noun to common noun or even verb ("googled" anyone lately?). Consider some of the words that started life as proprietary names: *cellophane, granola, jungle gym, martini, minivan, novocaine, pablum, pancake makeup, xerox.* The list goes on.

Names don't just represent brands; they *start* brands. The ideas and feelings that a name evokes provide the scaffolding for a brand. Consider the name Google. Even if you don't know it's based on *googol*, a word coined by a child for a very large number, you probably get a playful, almost goofy vibe from it. Maybe you associate it (consciously or not) with the cartoon character Barney Google, the expression "googly eyes," or representations of baby talk like "goo goo ga ga." Now think of how well that vibe goes with Google's simple interface, the primary colors of its logo, and its reputation as a fun and creative place to work. Now try to imagine the same logo and reputation being associated with the name Microsoft. Microsoft countered Google's playfulness with a fun search engine name of its own: Bing.

Of course, many names are new coined words (or phrases). Most are created using the same processes that give birth to other new words. People combine existing words, and parts of words, to create new words. Take the word *job*, stick on the suffix *-ster*, and you've got the name Jobster. Blend the words *technology* and *literati* (or *digerati*) and you've got the name Technorati. And so on.

Usually people take the raw material of our natural shared language to construct artificial words, but today's linguistic environment is so crowded with artificial words that they've become part of the raw material. Take the name Jobdango. Why is that dang *-dango* ending dangling there? You could argue that this name blends *job* and *fandango*, the name of a dance. But there's really no sensible motivation for such a blend. Rather, this name seems to be a blend of *job* and the *name* Fandango, for a website that sells movie tickets. The name Fandango is based on the word for the dance, but it's kind of a pun, because the site is for movie *fans*. Jobdango seems to be sort of a nod to the movie ticket site; it says, "I'm like Fandango for jobs."

So the artificial word *Fandango*, based on the natural word *fandango*, becomes the raw material for the artificial word *Jobdango*. The artificial is built out of the artificial. It's like what you find in music with sampling, or in food with the Dairy Queen Blizzard, which uses candy bars as raw ingredients in milkshakes. And now *-dango* has taken on a life of its own, appearing in names like Handango, Zoodango, and even GodDango. It has become what linguists call a *cranberry morpheme*, a meaningless word part that, like *cran-*, is left when you chop a meaningful part off a word.

The *-dango* phenomenon shows the historical process of language change being initiated and accelerated through naming. It invites another analogy to biological evolution: naming is to language change as breeding is to evolutionary change in domestic animals. Humans speed up and direct the process of evolution by selecting for traits that they like in their animal companions—random variation and artificial selection, if you will. It's similar with naming. For the most part it works with word formation strategies that lead to language change organically but accelerate the process through conscious human choice. The emergence of the *-dango* cranberry morpheme is a good example. It's possible to imagine a historical scenario in which the name Fandango is reanalyzed by speakers as including the word *fan*, and that leads to the emergence of the *-dango* suffix in an organic way.

Where will this process lead? The crowded space of names might create a need for more complex ways to create names. A blend, for example, is normally made out of just two seamlessly combined words, but it can be made out of three. The second part of the name Bare Escentuals manages to combine the words *essential*, *scent*, and *sensual*. A company in Seattle is called Fabjectory, which is a blend of *fabject* and *object*. But *fabject* itself is a blend of *fabricated* and *object*, coined by science fiction writer Bruce Sterling. This is a complicated name, but complexity is a natural adaptation to a challenging environment.

THE VERBAL REAL ESTATE MARKET

Just how competitive is the space of names? In 2006 there were already more than six million businesses in the United States (and more than half a million new ones were created that year alone). Of course, every one of them has a name.

The US Patent and Trademark Office has over a million and a half active trademark registrations, and more than 350,000 new registrations were filed in 2009. To put that into perspective, by some estimates the average English-speaking adult knows about 40,000 words. The number of active US trademarks is more than thirty times larger than the common English vocabulary (and the number of existing business names is about six times the number of active trademarks).

As daunting as the number of business names and trademarks

is, things look even worse when you consider the web. Naming is no longer just for corporate marketing departments and entrepreneurs who invest their life savings in a business. It's for everyone with an interest in personal branding. And that's everyone. This is the age of blogs, micro-startups, and eBay stores run by people in their pajamas. All these projects need names.

This universal participation makes naming more difficult than ever. The web is now a crucial marketing platform, and naming means finding available Internet domain names. The vast universe of existing domain names makes it difficult to be both meaningful and distinctive.

Internet infrastructure company VeriSign reports that by the fourth quarter of 2009, over eighty million ".com" domains were registered and 192 registrations across all the top-level domains (".org," ".net," etc.), with about eleven million new registrations made in the last quarter of 2009. According to Technorati CEO David Sifry's report "The State of the Live Web" for 2007, there were more than seventy million blogs, and 120,000 new ones were created every day.

As the forces driving the artificial growth of our vocabulary grow stronger, things are looking bright for neologism.

16

MAKE A PLAY ON WORDS

Sometimes coining a new word means making a play on an existing word. Farecast, the original name for Bing Travel, a service that predicts airfares, is a play on *forecast*. The name Gnomedex is a comical play on the name Comdex, which was once a popular technology conference.

Wordplay is a staple of songwriters as well as copywriters. John Lennon and Paul McCartney (especially Lennon) were lovers of wordplay, and that's apparent in much of the Beatles' work. Two of their pivotal albums, which some critics place among the most influential in rock history, use wordplay in their titles. *Rubber Soul* is of course a play on the phrase *rubber sole*, a type of shoe sole. As Beatles lore has it, Paul McCartney heard a black musician describe Mick Jagger's singing as "plastic soul," which he interpreted to mean 'white people's soul,' and that inspired the pun. And *Revolver* seems to be an aggressive reference to a weapon, but it can also be a fanciful description of an LP on a turntable. And let's not forget that the name Beatles itself is a play on the words *beat* and *beetles*. Lennon really cut loose with word-play of another sort in his book *In His Own Write*. Here's what he wrote in his "About the Awful" section on the back:

> *As far as I'm conceived this correction of short writty is the most wonderful larf I've ever ready.*

Rough going unless you *really* love wordplay.

A good play on words, like any coinage, must respect the normal cadences of speech and the sounds of the words used as raw material in a coinage. It's surprising how many new words fail to do that.

Consider this headline from *BusinessWeek*: "The New E-spionage Threat." The coined word *e-spionage* refers to spying that takes place over the Internet. Saying this word out loud almost hurts. The word *espionage* has a short *e* that grabs the following *s* and makes it part of the first syllable. The long *e* in *e-spionage* makes a whole syllable by itself, so the *s* becomes part of the second syllable, which is pronounced "spee." The result sounds awkward and silly. This would be "eye wordplay," similar to eye rhyme and eye ambiguity.

Another poorly constructed word is *Defeatocrats*—the epithet that former White House Press Secretary Tony Snow coined in 2006 to characterize Democratic opposition to the war in Iraq. Conservative bloggers echoed the term for a while. Liberal bloggers proposed some terrible rejoinders, one of which was *Republicants*.

Neither of these new words really caught on. One reason is their poor construction. *Defeatocrat* sounds like a random school-yard insult, largely because there's no linguistic or conceptual motivation for replacing the first single syllable of *Democrat* with the two-syllable word *defeat*, apart from Snow's desire to make the Democrats look weak.

Republicant might elicit a brief chuckle, but it falls flat because the final syllable of *Republican* just isn't pronounced emphatically the way the word *can't* should be here. This is one of the most common causes of failed wordplay—syllable stress mismatch, which I christened *awkwordplay* in the preceding chapter. The names Carticipate, Mapufacture, Syncplicity, and Teensurance all contain one-syllable words (*car, map, sync, teen*). In any playful coinage like this, people would expect the one-syllable words to be stressed, but in these names, they replace unstressed syllables of longer words. The results sound strained and unpleasant.

Wordplay occurs in slogans as well as names. Amtrak tells us to SEE AMERICA AT SEE LEVEL. (In a failed attempt at similar wordplay, the movie *Ghost Ship* used the tagline SEA EVIL, which doesn't make much sense or sound natural under either interpretation.) Nabisco asks us, WHY SNACKRIFICE? Picking up on the snack food industry's penchant for wordplay, the *Onion* reported that

FRITOLAYSIA CUTS OFF CHIPLOMATIC RELATIONS WITH

SNAKISTAN

This playful headline from 2005 prefigured the much-publicized "snacklish" ad campaign for Snickers, created in 2009 by TBWA/Chiat/Day. The campaign was based completely on wordplay, featuring invented words such as *hungerectomy* and *satisfectellent*.

Plays on words can be based on spelling. The email service Xobni is *inbox* spelled backward. The name Hotmail was originally HoTMaiL, based on *HTML*. Tputh, the name of an online news magazine for "geeks, designers, and venture capitalists," was inspired partly by the Cyrillic spelling of *Pravda*'s English equivalent.

Publishers have really taken to wordplay in their book titles. There is, of course, the wildly successful *Freakonomics*, and its sequel *Super Freakonomics* (you can almost hear Rick James singing, "It's super freaky!"). Other recent titles include *Shoptimism* and *Moregasm*.

Many noncommercial neologisms are instances of wordplay. Instead of controversies, newspapers sometimes like to write about *nontroversies*—things that seem really urgent for a day or two, and then . . . wait, what were we talking about? And we don't just have activists anymore—we also have *Blacktivists* and *hacktivists*. Rolf Sten Andersen proposed the following neologism on Twitter:

> *Fauxboes: The annoying kids on Haight Street that endlessly harass you for money.*
> — *@RSAndersen, quoted in* Twitter Wit

Sometimes words are toys. Add a little playtime to your microstyle.

17

COMBINE WORDS ARTFULLY

When we put together a simple phrase or a noun compound, we have to not only choose words, but decide which words go together. Words are like ingredients, and when you combine them, you can create dishes that have never existed before.

In the late 1970s a guy named Eric met a guitarist through a music store ad and formed the politically confrontational band the Dead Kennedys. Thinking, perhaps, that Eric was not an outrageous enough stage name for the lead singer of such a band, he became known as Jello Biafra.

The name Jello Biafra is a masterpiece of microstyle, a testament to the power that the juxtaposition of two simple words can unleash. *Jello* is, of course, the genericized trademark for a gelatin dessert product (Jell-O). *Biafra* was the name of a secessionist state in Nigeria in the 1960s. If you know about Biafra, you can't see these two words together without thinking about the huge disparities between life in the United States and in the rest of the world. Jello is highly processed and nutritionally frivolous—food as a toy.

Biafra was a place where tens of thousands of people starved to death because of a military blockade during the Nigerian Civil War. Combining those two ideas makes one uncomfortably aware of the grotesque excesses of American life, and that was part of Eric's point.

Not all new verbal dishes are as pungent as Jello Biafra. Consider the name Blue Flavor, for a Seattle web design firm. This simple two-word combination evokes an idea that's far more unusual and intriguing than the meaning of either component word alone.

To interpret any phrase like this, we start with the words and then figure out how to fit their meanings together. The words themselves help with this process. Some words exist just to combine with others in certain ways; they give our brains instructions, so to speak, about how to begin the meaning construction process. In this case, the adjective *blue*, occurring before a noun, tells us that it should modify the noun—change its meaning in a certain way. The noun *flavor* violates our expectations in this regard. Color words modify words for things that have colors, such as *wall*, *chair*, or *shirt*. *Flavor* is not such a word.

Let's try indirect association (*metonymy*) to interpret this name. Colors don't literally have flavor, but there are certain canonical color-flavor associations. Makers of jelly beans, slushy drinks, and other artificially colored foods use these all the time. Yellow for lemon. Purple for grape. Red for cherry or strawberry. Orange for orange, of course. Green for lime or mint or maybe green apple. But missing from this list is blue. In his monologue for the very first episode of *Saturday Night Live*, the late, great George Carlin bemoaned the absence of blue food. Even blueberries, he observed, are "blue on the vine, purple on the plate."

Blue Flavor names a mythical taste that doesn't exist. Something you've never experienced before. It's a great idea for a web design studio to evoke, and it shows the power of putting words—even just two of them—together.

Surprising word combinations aren't just for punk rockers and web designers. Recall the compound "Jesus rifles" used in the headline discussed in Chapter 1. A compound or phrase gives you an opportunity to create new meaning, to make your message more than the sum of its parts. Some messages represent lost opportunities. Consider the name for a company that wants to build an elevator that goes into outer space. An elevator to space—pretty cool, right? The name is LiftPort. Lifting is carrying, porting is carrying, a lift is a kind of conveyance, a port is a place of departure. Combining these words hits the same overly general and uninspiring meanings again and again, neglecting more interesting ideas like outer space, science fiction, and doing the impossible.

Compounds are very common in English and come naturally to people. There are a few things to keep in mind, however, when creating them. The most important is that the second word in the compound will be interpreted as the "head"—the word with the key meaning that will represent the category of the compound as a whole. An airport is a type of a port, not a type of air, and the White House is a type of house, not a kind of white. This may be intuitively obvious, but I've often observed people ignoring this fact when they tackle the naming challenge by generating long lists of randomly combined words.

Since the second word is the head, the first one is typically a modifier. That means it will modify, or change, the meaning of the head in some way. It's important to pick a word that's up to the task. There aren't many grammatical constraints to worry about here; concern yourself with what makes sense.

While phrases represent a step up in complexity from compounds, phrase making is still built on word selection and therefore on the kind of framing that words can achieve. For example, in 2008 the US Justice Department announced a new initiative to get tough on *tax defiers*. These are people, previously known as *tax protesters*, who question the legal validity of federal taxation and refuse to file taxes. The new phrase *tax defiers* accomplishes two things. First, it grabs attention because it's unfamiliar. Second, it completely reframes the activity of the people in question. The word *protesters* evokes the idea of people exercising their constitutional rights to fight for a just cause. The word *defiers*, on the other hand, implies people who stubbornly resist just authority. Parents talk about their children being *defiant* when they refuse to go to bed or clean up after themselves.

Titles of movies and books sometimes put words together in surprising ways to present intriguing or fanciful ideas. Gus Van Sant made a great film about small-time crooks and drug addicts in the 1970s Pacific Northwest. He called it *Drugstore Cowboy*. Not two words you'd expect to find together (unless you happened to be at Wall Drug in South Dakota), but the title referred to the Matt Dillon and Kelly Lynch characters' freewheeling lifestyle and penchant for robbing drugstores to score barbiturates. The book and movie *A Clockwork Orange* uses part of an old cockney expression to evoke the surreal world it depicts.

Incongruous word combinations can also be played for laughs. Here's a headline from the *Onion*:

CASES OF GLITTER LUNG ON THE RISE AMONG
ELEMENTARY-SCHOOL ART TEACHERS

The heart of this joke is, of course, the phrase "glitter lung," which bears a vague resemblance to "black lung," the name of a serious condition that miners suffer as a result of inhaling coal dust. The dark humor of the *Onion* headline plays on the implicit comparison between miners, who work in dark, gloomy, and dangerous conditions, and elementary school teachers, who work in rooms filled with toys, primary colors, and children. The phrase "glitter lung" expressed this comparison in miniature.

Sometimes a simple word combination, or even a combination of a prefix and a word, serves as a euphemism for a more familiar word in a lame attempt to make something bad look good—to put lipstick on a pig, if you will. Have you noticed that it's hard to buy a used car nowadays? That's because cars are no longer used, they're "pre-owned." *Used* implies used up, while the term *pre-owned* suggests that someone has kindly gone to the trouble of testing out ownership of a vehicle to ensure that everything's OK. The most ridiculous euphemism I've encountered lately is *pre-reclined*, used by Spirit Airlines to describe the nonadjustable seats in its new Airbus A320s. Just imagine a flight attendant dealing with a confused customer asking how to make his seat go down: "Sir, our seats are pre-reclined, which means you're already comfortable!"

Combining words is really about combining concepts. Doing that well means paying attention to what makes sense, avoiding redundancy, and creating interesting juxtapositions.

18

USE GRAMMAR
EXPRESSIVELY

One of the surest signs that we've entered the era of the micromessage has been the emergence of a new comedy genre: the fake newspaper headline. The *Onion*, which has provided many of the examples in this book, is a veritable humor factory that began as a small campus publication in Madison, Wisconsin. It built its empire largely on the strength of its satirical headlines. It has articles as well, but they're usually extended riffs on a basic concept that's expressed best in headline form. The front page of its news publication also features headlines for stories that don't even exist. The headlines are where the action is. That makes the *Onion*'s style of humor perfect for Twitter, where it had more than two million followers when I wrote this.

The *Onion* manages to crank out reliably funny headlines again and again, despite (or perhaps because of) the fact that it uses obvious formulas to do it. One formula combines an ancient rhetorical trope with the abbreviated syntactic conventions of newspaper headlines. This is the basis for what may be the *Onion*'s trademark move: combining zeugma with a conjunction that uses a comma instead of the word "and." *Zeugma* is the technique, recognized and named by the ancient Greeks, of using a word (usually a verb) with two phrases—such as two direct objects—that require different interpretations of the word in question.

A classic example, CLINTON FEELS NATION'S PAIN, BREASTS, calls upon *feel* to refer both to emotional experience and to palpation. Bill Clinton, a master of expressing empathy with the American electorate, had become strongly associated with his catchphrase "I feel your pain." He was also known as a seductive charmer and an adulterer.

Here's another *Onion* headline:

NATION'S DOG OWNERS DEMAND TO KNOW WHO'S
A GOOD BOY

The silliness of this headline depends on the clause following the word *know*. While the first part of the headline, "Nation's Dog Owners Demand to Know," implies an emphatic desire for answers, "Who's a Good Boy" is a completely content-free rhetorical question that people use to praise their pets.

Satirical headlines are great for a linguist because they often rely on clever syntactic devices. They're nice demonstrations of the fact that grammar is expressive. That basic fact about language was buried beneath piles of anxiety during the era of Big Style. Ordinary people got the idea that grammar equals rules, right and wrong. But putting words together into a sentence isn't like arranging flatware correctly for a formal dinner. Grammar works together with words to express nuances of meaning.

Every conventional grammatical pattern, whether "correct" or not, has some reason to exist. Some rules of style would lead you to believe that isn't the case. For example, many people have been instructed not to use the passive voice in their writing. This might be a problem of branding: who wants their writing to be "passive" when it can be "active"? But the poor, beleaguered passive actually performs a valuable public service. It's not just a trick that wrongdoers use to conceal responsibility for their deeds; it's not just about saying, "Mistakes were made" instead of "I made mistakes." The passive helps us keep the focus on the important characters and props in a story, and it saves us from having to introduce new but insignificant characters without any context. If everyone wants to know what's become of the jewels, it's more relevant to say, "They've been stolen," treating the topic as the grammatical subject, than it is to say, "Someone stole them."

Being careful about constructing phrases has more to do with recognizing their communicative functions than with being "correct." Know why you're using the ones you pick rather than the alternatives. Little grammatical differences can make a big difference.

Consider the McDonald's slogan ɪ'ᴍ ʟᴏᴠɪɴ' ɪᴛ! What if it used the same words but different grammar: "I love it!" How boring is that? But why does "I'm lovin' it" feel so different from "I love it"? It turns out there's a lot going on with that little *-ing* ending. "I love it" is a simple statement of opinion. The default way to express opinions about things is to use verbs that occur in the simple present tense and express states: "I like this," "I hate that," and so forth. "I'm lovin' it" is something you'd say while actually in the process of enjoying something. It turns the emotion verb *love* into something more like an action verb. It also turns an expression of opinion, which might be uttered at any time, into a situationally specific utterance, one that conjures up a particular context and a particular activity. It puts you right there at McDonald's (or at least, holding a carry-out bag in your lap), with ketchup on your face and greasy, salty fingers.

Think of a group of semantically related words that you might expect to occur in similar grammatical contexts. For example, consider nouns for emotions we feel about other people: *fondness, love, anger, annoyance*. That's a pretty specific category. Yet these words occur in different phrases. We "fall in love," but we don't "fall in fondness" or "fall in anger." We feel "love for" someone, but we feel "anger toward" someone.

Since phrasal contexts can be so specific to individual words, it's possible to evoke a word simply by using the phrase pattern that normally accompanies it. That can be an interesting source of wordplay. For example, the Metallica song "St. Anger" includes the line "I'm madly in anger with you." The word *anger* occupies a syntactic context that's normally reserved for the word *love*, so we're invited to find parallels between the two emotions. This lyric alludes to language that's not there through the artful use of syntax.

The movie title *A Slight Case of Murder* works in a similar way. An old J&B Scotch ad used the slogan SCOTCH AND THE SINGLE GIRL, an obvious reference to the 1962 novel *Sex and the Single Girl*, by Helen Gurley Brown, who later became editor in chief of *Cosmopolitan* magazine. The slogan appeared over an image of three women: one blonde, one brunette, and one redhead (a straight-white-male fantasy vision of diversity, circa 1971). Without using the word *sex*, J&B Scotch managed to imply that its product might have something to do with both "single girls" and sex. As an appeal to women, this slogan said, "Scotch, like sex, is one of the forbidden pleasures to which you are entitled." As an appeal to men, it said, "Liberated single girls will drink our Scotch and have sex with you." But, you know, in a classy, discreet way.

Countless breweries have used the slogan THE BEER THAT MADE MILWAUKEE JEALOUS—an allusion to the Schlitz beer slogan THE BEER THAT MADE MILWAUKEE FAMOUS. This is an especially natural allusion, since *famous* and *jealous* end with rhyming syllables.

Some allusions strain credibility. When Mars, Incorporated

sold one of its candy bars with the slogan A MARS BAR A DAY HELPS YOU WORK, REST AND PLAY, it implied an implausible health benefit by evoking the old saying "An apple a day keeps the doctor away."

RIDING THE ELEVATOR

Pitching, discussed in Chapter 1, requires the resourceful use of verbal tools, including grammar. The world of pitching is characterized by fierce competition for the attention, approval, and money of a few powerful people. Because those people are so busy, would-be pitchers must be prepared to take advantage of the smallest opportunity, the briefest moment, to describe their proposal. And that means crafting perfect phrases.

The Hollywood high-concept pitch—an extremely short phrase that encapsulates a movie, often by comparing it to another movie—must wring all the meaning it can from a simple phrase. And high-concept pitches are not limited to the movie industry. First-time author Patricia Wood secured a six-figure contract for her novel *Lottery* with the following pitch: FORREST GUMP WINS POWERBALL. Startups use high-concept pitches to get the attention of venture capitalists. Many new search tools are pitched as GOOGLE FOR _____ . In fact, Barack Obama, in the first presidential campaign debate of 2008, pitched an idea to the American public as GOOGLE FOR GOVERNMENT.

In an article titled "High Concept Defined Once and For All," screenwriter and producer Steve Kaire, who has successfully pitched several big-budget moves and lectures on the art of the pitch, makes it clear that "high concept" is not just a type of pitch but a type of project: "Only High Concept projects can be sold from a pitch because they are pitch driven." If you want to be able to sell a movie from a pitch, it makes sense to start with the pitch and work backward. An essentially verbal constraint—that your pitch be no longer than a sentence—serves as an important filter in the whole process of making movies and, perhaps increasingly, of publishing books and starting companies.

The high-concept pitch takes various forms, but it almost always involves evoking an existing movie, book, or company, and then indicating how yours would be *different*. Mentioning an existing company or movie is really the only way to convey a whole plot or a whole business plan using only part of a small phrase. A common form for these statements is to use the title or company name and modify it with a phrase—typically a prepositional phrase—that indicates a different realm in which the standard of comparison must be reimagined. Sometimes the reimagining is simple. GOOGLE FOR GOVERNMENT would obviously be a Google-like search engine that would help us find information about laws and other government documents.

Sometimes the reimagining is more complicated. To make sense of JAWS IN SPACE, the tagline for the movie *Alien*, you have to take everything you know about *Jaws* and everything you know about space, and then figure out how *Jaws* would have to be different to work in space. OK, in space there wouldn't be a shark, so the alien must play that role. And since the most suspenseful moments of *Jaws* take place on and near a boat, there must be something like that in *Alien*: a spaceship.

Believe it or not, there's a cognitive theory of the pitch. Well, not of the pitch per se, but of the kinds of little phrases that are used to compare pitched ideas to existing ones, like JAWS IN SPACE. It's the theory of *conceptual blending*, which has been developed by cognitive scientist Gilles Fauconnier and cognitive literary theorist Mark Turner. Conceptual blending theory is based on Fauconnier's concept of mental spaces, which uses a spatial metaphor to represent different concepts and the relations between them. Consider the following sentence: "When I was in college, I had a lot more hair." To make sense of this sentence, you form a sort of image of me now and an image of me in college, and you "see" that the college me has more hair than the current me. You can think of these images corresponding to different times of my life as spaces. You might even squish these images together, so the college me and the real me are standing next to each other and are easy to compare. That would be a blended space, and an example of conceptual blending.

In Fauconnier and Turner's view, blended spaces can be sources of new insights. To show this, they like to use the example of the Riddle of the Buddhist Monk, which is really more of a brainteaser. Here's the setup: At sunrise a Buddhist monk starts walking up the side of a mountain. He arrives at the top at sundown, and spends the night there. Then at sunrise the next day, he sets off down the mountain, following the same path, and arrives at the bottom at sunset. Now, here's the riddle: Is there one place on the path that the monk occupies at exactly the same time on both days? If so, how can you prove it?

The solution to this riddle is easy if you make a blended space. Imagine that there are two monks and they make their trips on the same day, one starting from the bottom of the mountain and one starting from the top. Common sense tells you that the monks will pass each other, and at that exact time they'll be at the same place on the path.

This riddle shows us how combining concepts in certain ways can lead to new knowledge, ideas, and insights. The little comparative phrases we find in high-concept pitches might not hamper creativity, but rather be sources of creativity. In the expressive power of phrases are the seeds of ideas.

19

REPEAT STRUCTURES

A common way to give messages balance and rhythm is to repeat phrasal structures. This technique is called *structural parallelism*, *parallel construction*, or just *parallelism*, and it is especially common in political oratory. John F. Kennedy famously said to all Americans, "Ask not what your country can do for you. Ask what you can do for your country." Barack Obama made liberal use of parallelism in his inaugural address. He began his speech this way:

> *My fellow citizens: I stand here today . . .*
> *humbled by the task before us,*
> *grateful for the trust you have bestowed,*
> *mindful of the sacrifices borne by our ancestors.*

Notice the repetition of adjectives in *humbled*, *grateful*, *mindful*, each followed by a prepositional phrase. Charles Dickens's novel *A Tale of*

Two Cities begins with a well-known series of parallel statements:

> *It was the best of times, it was the worst of times; it was the*
> *age of wisdom, it was the age of foolishness; it was the epoch*
> *of belief, it was the epoch of incredulity; it was the season of*
> *Light, it was the season of Darkness; it was the spring of hope,*
> *it was the winter of despair; we had everything before us, we*
> *had nothing before us; we were all going directly to Heaven,*
> *we were all going the other way.*

Structural parallelism exists in less highfalutin contexts as well. The news cliché "from Wall Street to Main Street" contains two prepositional phrases whose objects are built on the word *street*. The constructional idiom we saw earlier, the one that gives us expressions like "the bigger they are, the harder they fall" and "the more, the merrier" has parallelism built right into it. Republican vice presidential candidate Sarah Palin used structural parallelism when she uttered this sound bite about Barack Obama during the 2008 campaign: "He's not willing to drill for energy but he's sure willing to drill for votes." Heidi Klum uses the same catchphrase every time she steps onto the catwalk in the TV show *Project Runway*:

One day you are in, and the next day you are out.

Parallelism is used as a structuring device in six-word memoirs:

In Florida. In Debt. In Love.
> *—Jules1982*, Smith Magazine, *February 28, 2010*

Heart in SF. Arm in Viet Nam.
> *—Harlan Stanton, IACIAI (quoted in* It All Changed
> in an Instant: More Six-Word Memoirs*)*

Parallelism can be an accomplice to wordplay, especially when it involves repeating words. At the end of the Disney/Pixar animated film *The Incredibles*, a villain who looks like a monstrous mole dressed as a coal miner bursts through the ground on a giant drilling machine and shouts "I am the Underminer! I'm always beneath you, but nothing's beneath me!" Here the word *beneath* is used first in a literal sense, to describe a physical location, and then in a metaphorical idiom, describing a moral position. CompUSA's slogan—WE GOT IT. WE GET IT.—achieves a similar effect. A character in the movie *Monsters vs Aliens* says "I may not have a brain, but I have an idea."

Parallelism is a common feature of slogans:

I AM STUCK ON BAND-AID, AND BAND-AID'S STUCK ON ME.

BETTER BUILT, BETTER BACKED. *(Mitsubishi)*

GOOD FOOD. GOOD LIFE. *(Nestle)*

TOUCHING LIVES, IMPROVING LIFE. *(Proctor & Gamble)*

EXPECT MORE, PAY LESS. *(Target)*

YOU CAN DO IT. WE CAN HELP. *(The Home Depot)*

THE MORE YOU EAT, THE MORE YOU WANT. *(Cracker Jack, ca. 1919)*

WHEN IT RAINS, IT POURS. *(Morton Salt)*

IT'S NOT TV, IT'S HBO.

FLY LIKE A CEO, PAY LIKE A TEMP. *(Virgin America)*

DOUBLE YOUR PLEASURE, DOUBLE YOUR FUN, WITH DOUBLEMINT, DOUBLEMINT, DOUBLEMINT GUM.

BRING OUT THE HELLMANN'S AND BRING OUT THE BEST.

HAVE A BREAK. HAVE A KIT-KAT. *(J. Walter Thompson, 1957)*

KILL THE GERMS. FEEL THE CLEAN. *(Listerine)*

The parallelism of HBO's slogan has two components. First, there's the repeated clause structure—*it* followed by the linking verb *be* followed by a noun phrase (though the first clause is negated and the second isn't). Then there's the parallel between the two abbreviations: TV and HBO. The slogan distinguishes HBO from TV while establishing it as something of equal or greater importance.

Parallelism is often used to make comparisons; it can be the verbal equivalent of making a tipping-scale gesture with your hands. That makes it a kind of syntactic iconicity. The similarity in structure of the two (or more) parts in a case of parallelism shows a kind of equivalence or comparability in meaning. In the idiom that we see in "the more, the merrier," it's as if there are two scales measuring two separate quantities or levels of intensity, but they're linked. When one goes up, the other goes up.

Parallelism is usually accompanied by a key semantic relationship between contrasting words. They might be opposites, as in Target's slogan, EXPECT MORE, PAY LESS; or near-opposites, as in THE MORE YOU EAT, THE MORE YOU WANT; or they might be near-synonyms with a twist: WE GOT IT. WE GET IT. (the same word used in different grammatical forms and different meanings) or WHEN IT RAINS, IT POURS. (near-synonyms, but with a double meaning).

The point of parallelism is to give a message balance and rhythm. The two (or more) parts of the message should be similar in length and meter, and should have complementary meanings. The 1953 slogan THOSE WHO WANT THE FINEST WANT—THE STANDARD OF THE WORLD! seems both unbalanced and redundant.

Parallelism is the syntactic equivalent of the poetic patterns we saw in Chapter 12. It's a comforting form of repetition that adds an extra dimension to our short messages.

20

TEACH AN OLD CLICHÉ
NEW TRICKS

The late William Safire once came up with a list of "rules for writers," each of which amusingly broke itself. One was "avoid clichés like the plague." This is one of the most common pieces of advice writers get. Writing is supposed to be interesting, and interesting usually means fresh and different.

Of course, to avoid a cliché you need to know one when you see one. For instance, was that a cliché I just used? To "know one when you see one"? What is a cliché, really? It's a little piece of overused, prefab language. But our verbal landscape is filled with snippets of this kind of language. I'm not talking about words. There are idioms galore—conventional turns of phrase with specific meanings. These expressions do real work. Communication would be difficult without them.

One thing that makes a true cliché unappealing is that it's unnecessary. To "avoid clichés like the plague" just means to *really* avoid them. The strength and specificity of the image is out of proportion to the meager information it contributes. A cliché like this works against economy of expression.

If you think you might be using a cliché, try paraphrasing. If the paraphrase is shorter than your original phrasing and loses nothing important, then you probably had a cliché (on your hands). If the paraphrase is much longer, you might be better off with the shorter and more conventional phrasing. If I try to paraphrase "know one when you see one" (six syllables), I get "know how to identify one" (eight syllables) or "know how to recognize one" (seven syllables). Maybe I could have used "know how to spot one" (five syllables). We have to learn to distinguish between a cliché that's truly tired—one that's motivated by laziness rather than a desire to communicate—and idioms that do real work by communicating in a shorthand way.

Idioms aren't the only conventional expressions in our language; they're just the most unusual. Some simple, normal phrases sound familiar because we've all heard them a million times. Consider Nike's slogan JUST DO IT. Such phrases certainly aren't used for their originality. It's their conventionality that gives them their power.

If you've ever taken an introductory linguistics course, you've almost certainly been told about the wonderful productivity of language—the way it can be shaped into unique phrases and sentences to express thoughts that have never before been expressed. This versatility gives language its power as a vehicle of culture and thought. In the mainstream theories of grammar that were taught for decades, here's how that productivity was typically modeled: Here's a bag of words, and here's a bunch of abstract rules that you use to put them together. You can put the words together any way you want, as long as you follow the rules.

That approach provides plenty of flexibility to account for all the sentences that people do or might produce. As a model of the way people actually talk, though, it's unrealistic. It vastly overestimates the creativity that goes into the average sentence. Idioms, clichés, and other formulaic phrases suffuse ordinary discourse. I don't mean you run into one now and then. I mean they're *everywhere*.

Some genres of speech are notoriously cliché riddled. When athletes are interviewed after sporting events, they often give pat answers: "We brought our A-game," "It was a team effort," "They out-hustled us," etc. Politicians regularly throw out key phrases like treats for hungry constituents. When their answers are evasive or incoherent, those phrases really stick out as non sequiturs. Sarah Palin's ill-fated interview with Katie Couric during the 2008 presidential race provides an extreme example. Couric asked Palin whether she supported a $700 billion bailout of the financial industry, and here's what Palin said (Some of the conventional phrases she used are un-italicized for emphasis):

> *That's why I say I, like every American I'm speaking with, we're ill about this position that we have been put in where it is the taxpayers looking to bail out. But ultimately what the bailout does is help those who are concerned about the* health care reform *that is needed to help* shore up our economy. *Helping the—it's got to be all about* job creation *too,* shoring up our economy *and* putting it back on the right track. *So* health care reform *and* reducing taxes *and* reining in spending *has got to accompany* tax reductions *and* tax relief for Americans *and trade—we've got to see* trade as opportunity, *not as a competitive, scary thing, but one in five jobs being created in the trade sector today—we've got to look at that as more opportunity.*

Palin had been through some crash media training before her interview, and clearly these phrases are the little scraps she retained from her talking points; she used them as if she didn't even know what they meant. What do health care reform, job creation, reducing taxes, reining in spending, and "trade as opportunity" have to do with the financial bailout that Couric asked about? That's not clear. Palin even listed three paraphrases as if they were different things: "*reducing taxes* . . . has got to accompany *tax reductions* and *tax relief for Americans*." This is political discourse run amok.

Clichés and idioms are part of everyone's language. That's painfully obvious to any adult who attempts to learn a second language: even when you have the vocabulary and the rules down, you can still have lots of trouble understanding and being understood.

The familiarity of phrases can be a real asset in a micromessage. While conventional phrases can't express fresh concepts the way a phrase like Blue Flavor does, they're unmatched at evoking conversational contexts. Nike's slogan JUST DO IT is a great example. This is a phrase that you can easily imagine hearing from a coach or saying to yourself. Just as words evoke frames, familiar phrases evoke imagined conversations that give them their special resonance. We don't need to completely avoid them, as long as we can find an interesting way to use them. Safire found a great way to use "like the plague," after all, though it may be hard to reproduce.

Taking a familiar phrase and plopping it into an unfamiliar context can give it new meaning and make it fresh. In this situation we really see the relevance principle at work. The Burger King slogan HAVE IT YOUR WAY is a good example. People normally use the phrase when conceding an argument about a course of action: "OK, have it your way." Burger King used it in reference to its burgers—you get them cooked to order with toppings you choose. Bulova Accutron watches used the slogan EQUAL PAY, EQUAL TIME in 1972—the year the Equal Rights Amendment passed as a joint resolution in both houses of Congress. The implication, of course, was that women deserve expensive luxury watches as much as men do.

Sometimes phrases, like words, are poorly chosen. In 1973, American Airlines used the slogan REST, KEEP WARM, AND DRINK LIQUIDS—a cliché we expect to hear from a doctor. This was meant to suggest that American Airlines passengers would be pampered, but unfortunately it also suggested that they might be sick.

Recall the BECU credit union slogan that we saw in Chapter 9:

WE ARE TURNING THE FINANCIAL WORLD RIGHT SIDE UP.

This is a play on the cliché "turning X upside down." The idea behind that cliché is that in the business world it's good to be "disruptive," to shake things up. After the financial crisis of 2008–09, upside down was not looking so good. The slogan WE ARE TURNING THE FINANCIAL WORLD RIGHT SIDE UP is brilliant, because it points out the flawed thinking that lies behind the original cliché and promises a return to a normal stable state. It manages to be both satirical and comforting.

Simply calling attention to the oddness of an idiom can make it more interesting. In the Magnetic Fields song "Reno Dakota," which is full of playful rhymes and verbal gags, a jilted lover sings,

And yet you don't call me it's making me blue
Pantone 292

The use of the word *blue* to mean 'sad' is such an established cliché in American popular music that it's used in the name of America's signature musical form. "Pantone 292" is printers' code for a very specific blue. Tying the word to the context of color in such a literal and specific way makes it stand out. It also creates ironic distance between the songwriter's message and the idiom's meaning. It's hard to take the sadness of the song's protagonist seriously when it's expressed in a way that showcases form rather than meaning.

Some tweets employ a similar technique. Here are a couple examples from *Twitter Wit*:

Doc says I'm as healthy as a horse. Well, a horse that smokes. But still.

— *@sflovestory*

Change is inevitable, except from vending machines.
— *@Thedropofahat, quoted by davidbdale*

When we use idioms so often that they become clichés, the images and metaphors they evoke sometimes sink beneath the surface, so we no longer see them. Then, when something makes them resurface, they can surprise us with their strangeness. Hauling these odd underwater creatures up on the dock is one way to create a great one-liner.

Some of the funniest tweets I've come across use that technique. One Twitter user wrote,

The worst part about the gravy train is the abrupt stops.
— *@swamibooba, quoted in* Twitter Wit

This little masterpiece of microstyle gives us a very vivid image of sloshing, splashing gravy to highlight the inherent absurdity of the expression "gravy train." What's more, it's true: when the gravy train stops abruptly, it's unpleasant in the metaphorical sense as well as the literal sense.

Another user wrote,

Revenge is a dish best served a la mode.
— *@secretsquirrel, quoted in* Twitter Wit

This, of course, is a play on the expression "revenge is a dish best served cold," which has a clear metaphorical meaning: to really enjoy revenge, we should calmly plan it and savor it. @Secret-squirrel's gag plays with the logic of that metaphor. Since we know from another cliché that "revenge is sweet," it must be a dessert, and if a dessert is delicious served cold, surely it's even better with ice cream. The absurdity arises when we try to make sense of this image in the context of revenge; we're forced to mix the literal and the metaphorical and envision plots that somehow involve frozen dairy products.

A number of six-word memoirs on the *Smith Magazine* website play on conventional expressions:

> *Don't swing until your second marriage.*
> —*Larry D. Smith, December 31, 2007*

> *I came, I saw, I kvetched.*
> —*Josh_Neufeld, January 22, 2008*

> *Wake up, wash, rinse, and repeat.*
> —*laura, January 24, 2008*

> *Objects were closer than they appeared.*
> —*Michael_Grossman, February 4, 2008*

Twitter also sees its share of repurposed clichés, as these examples illustrate:

> *I fought the bra and the bra won.*
> — *@bliccy, quoted in* Twitter Wit

> *The creative department giveth, and the legal team taketh away.*
> — *@scarequotes, Twitter, February 2010*

One of my favorite techniques for revitalizing idioms is to use conventionally metaphorical expressions in contexts where they're literally true. Just to be fancy, let's call this *demetaphorization*. When using this technique, you get extra points if you can make both the literal and the metaphorical meaning relevant and apt; then you're exploiting ambiguity in a way that's magical rather than embarrassing (see Chapter 7).

Demetaphorization has been used in advertising slogans probably as long as there have been advertising slogans. The first major American advertising agency, N. W. Ayer & Son, used the technique in 1911 in one of the most famous slogans of all time: WHEN IT RAINS, IT POURS (for Morton Salt). Oddly, this famous example doesn't get the extra credit points for felicitous ambiguity, because the metaphorical meaning of this expression is negative: when things get bad, they get really bad. Nevertheless, demetaphorization is memorable because it reminds us of the vivid physical situations that are the foundation of many common figures of speech.

Here are some other examples. American Airlines used the slogan SOMETHING SPECIAL IN THE AIR, which is usually a metaphorical way to describe a positive shared mood, but in this case actually refers to airplanes as well. Continental, for its part, used WE REALLY MOVE OUR TAIL FOR YOU. Bisquick used the slogan SOMETHING GOOD ALWAYS COMES OF IT, which usually refers to an emotionally positive outcome, but in this case also refers to delicious biscuits or other baked goods. Hertz Rent a Car used LET HERTZ PUT YOU IN THE DRIVER'S SEAT. International Paper Company had the slogan WHERE GOOD IDEAS GROW ON TREES. Canon used the slogan IMAGE IS EVERYTHING. In this last case, again no extra credit, because the idiomatic meaning of this phrase implies a superficial attitude that a company would not necessarily want to adopt. Proclaiming "image is everything" might be considered an instance of strategically saying the wrong thing (see Chapter 9), making a provocative claim to get attention. The slogan is redeemed, of course, by the fact that Canon deals in literal rather than meta-phorical images.

Titles of books and films sometimes take a humdrum idiom or cliché and give it a special luster and resonance by putting it in the spotlight. It's similar to the way Marcel Duchamp high-lighted the artistic properties of everyday objects—most famously, a urinal—by hanging them as works of art in museums. Truman Capote did this when he took a legal term—"in cold blood"—and made it the title of his famous nonfiction novel. Movie titles that use this approach include *Boys Don't Cry*, *Shadow of a Doubt*, and *The Usual Suspects*.

The *Onion* constantly plays with news clichés to make pointed jokes. We've all seen headlines saying that some disaster "leaves thousands homeless." The *Onion* produced this headline:

MYSPACE OUTAGE LEAVES MILLIONS FRIENDLESS

This headline puts the word *friendless* absurdly into a context where you expect *homeless*, implying that friendships can be wiped out overnight the way physical structures can. The real genius of it, though, is that social networking friendships *can* be wiped out that easily, because they're not real. Putting the loss of a MySpace "friend" on the same level as losing the roof over your head really drives this message home.

Another *Onion* gem results from combining two conventional expressions involving the word *cost*—"cost of living" and "weigh-ing costs and benefits":

COST OF LIVING NOW OUTWEIGHS BENEFITS

Sometimes the web is less a conversation than it is a game of telephone. The same stories, jokes, and expressions are repeated again and again. This is why the blogosphere has sometimes also been referred to as the "echo chamber." A blog search on a particular topic will often turn up many posts that say essentially the same thing. It's similar to the way stories from newswires like the Associated Press make their way into countless local papers. In fact, just as bloggers are the new reporters, the original echo chamber was the world of newspaper reporting. Journalists often base their stories on other journalists' stories. Certain phrases so aptly capture important meanings that it's just not worth a busy journalist's time to rephrase them. As a result, phrases are repeated over and over until they become clichés.

The lean, mean little phrases that make it through this process often end up in headlines. Reporting on the fallout from the 2008 mortgage crisis and the collapse of investment bank Bear Stearns, the *New York Times* ran the following headline on March 21, 2008: ECONOMIC SQUEEZE MOVES FROM WALL ST. TO MAIN ST. If you Google the phrase "from Wall St. to Main St.," which we encountered in the previous chapter, you'll find quite a few occurrences.

What does this phrase mean and how does it work? It means the economic problem no longer affects only publicly traded corporations and large-scale investors but has begun to affect small businesses and consumers as well. This is an example of *metonymy* (introduced in Chapter 6): specific and vivid images of places stand for whole complex sectors of the economy with which those places are associated. This metonymy isn't limited to news reporting. Contrasting Wall Street with Main Street has become a common trope in political discourse.

In the first presidential debate between Barack Obama and John McCain in September 2008, each candidate used the trope twice:

OBAMA: *"Although we've heard a lot about Wall Street, those of you on Main Street I think have been struggling for a while."*

MCCAIN: *"We're not talking about failure of institutions on Wall Street. We're talking about failures on Main Street."*

OBAMA: *"We've had years in which the reigning economic ideology has been what's good for Wall Street, but not what's good for Main Street."*

MCCAIN: *"And Main Street is paying a penalty for the excesses and greed in Washington, DC, and on Wall Street."*

A similar phenomenon occurs with language on the web. When we click around and read stories here and there, we come across figures of speech and other little tropes that sometimes make their way into our own writing. All this is given an ironic twist by the fact that people who write on the web often feel the need to have a voice that's both entertaining and "real." This is especially noticeable on blogs. Through the subtle power of repetition and imitation, collective blogging efforts have created a sort of generic blogging voice that's anything but real. It's characterized by clichés and mannerisms that are intended to sound conversational. The use of texting abbreviations like OMG ("oh my god!") and LOL ("laughing out loud") and IMHO ("in my humble opinion") is just one example of this highly artificial "real" voice.

The blog Gawker published a list of forbidden blogging clichés at the end of 2006. In addition to texting abbreviations, it included artificial conversational pauses like "Um, . . ." and other attempts to mimic spoken language such as "Best. _____. Ever."— in which the periods suggest a halting pronunciation caused by breathless stupefaction.

Sometimes a cliché goes through so many different permutations that it becomes a sort of template. Consider the sentence "Will the last person to leave please turn out the lights?" This sentence most likely started life as an innocent sign in an office somewhere. Then people started using it metaphorically in reference to people leaving neighborhoods and companies. In the early 1970s, following big layoffs at Boeing in Seattle, someone put up a billboard that read, "Will the last person to leave Seattle please turn out the lights?" Then the variations started. Here are some examples that I found with a simple web search:

> *Will the last Akimbo employee please turn out the lights?*
> *Would the last democrat leaving South Africa please turn off the lights?*
> *Would the last Clinton campaigner please turn out the lights?*

And Clay Shirky on Twitter:

> *Jesus, will the last bank out of Wall Street please turn off the stock ticker?*
> — *@cshirky, September 17, 2008*

When an idiom cuts loose like this, it becomes what linguist David Crystal has called a *catch structure*, and what Glen Whitman, in response to an appeal by linguist Geoffrey Pullum, has called a *snowclone*. Writing on the blog Language Log in 2003, here's how Pullum defined this type of expression:

> *A multi-use, customizable, instantly recognizable, time-worn, quoted or misquoted phrase or sentence that can be used in an entirely open array of different jokey variants by lazy journalists and writers.*

Clichédom is the fate of micromessages that are too successful.

SOCIAL CONTEXT

Company slogans and political slogans, which often adopt an almost intimate tone, are examples of the way marketers pretend to have conversations with their markets. On the web, marketing has quite literally become conversational. That was the main point that Rick Levine, Christopher Locke, Doc Searls, and David Weinberger made in *The Cluetrain Manifesto*, first published on the web in 1999. *Cluetrain* urged marketers to adjust to a new business climate in which customers can easily talk back to companies and talk to one another about companies.

It's hard to overestimate the influence—or at least the prescience—of *Cluetrain*. If the web was already conversational in 1999, it has become exceedingly so with the explosive growth of social media such as blogs, wikis, and social networks. No web startup is complete without a blog, and virtually every company blog adopts a folksy, we're-normal-people-doing-our-best tone. It's the new orthodoxy for web marketing.

People have different names for it: "the participatory web," "the read/write web," "Web 2.0," etc. Whatever you call it, today's web differs from other media experiences because it supports interaction on a mass scale. Blog comment sections, discussion forums, and microblogging platforms such as Twitter essentially turn the web into one big cocktail party.

Microblogging, in particular, reproduces the sometimes awkward dynamics of parties to a surprising extent. Think about how conversation works at a party. You arrive and people are assembled into groups, but the groups blend into each other and people can move from one to another. Most of the groups gather around especially outgoing and entertaining individuals. When those individuals speak, they address themselves to a few people they can see close by and hear, but their comments are also heard by the "spectators" standing farther out where it's easy to listen but hard to get attention to speak. You wander around listening in on different conversations, deciding where you want to insert yourself. When you decide, you have to break in and get someone's attention in order to be heard.

For all but the most relaxed and outgoing people, this experience can involve some anxiety. For a long time the web offered a haven to people who have trouble in groups, giving the shy and socially awkward a comfortable way to communicate with others.

On Twitter and similar services, you can reproduce the anxiety of the cocktail party on the web. As a user, you potentially have "followers," who are simply people who choose to be able to hear what you say. (Whether or not they actually listen is another matter.) Some people have thousands of followers, and others have none at all. Some users "follow back," so the relationship is reciprocal; others don't, so they're talking without listening. You can choose to follow whomever you like, but they can choose to "block" you, preventing you from being able to read their updates. Anyone can choose to follow you, and unless you make a point of checking, you won't know which other people your followers are listening to at the same time.

Predictably, Twitter users tend to fall into two groups: those who make a play for attention, and those who are content to be wallflowers and make the occasional wisecrack for the benefit of close friends. For attention seekers, Twitter and other microblogging services offer a chance to be a wag. In the following tweet exchange quoted in *Twitter Wit*, note the quip by Twitter user @amandachapel:

> *I've had conversations with people I never would have met otherwise.*
>
> — *@lisahoffmann*

> *Like hanging out at the bus terminal.*
>
> — *@amandachapel*

Most tweets, however, do not approach this level. Some are held back by the sort of geeky inside jokes referring to web personalities and technology that are so common on the web:

> *Scoble is like a guest at a hotel for one, where a huge staff is trying to anticipate his every need. And he's angry.*
>
> — *@jayrosen_nyu*

There are two dimensions to social context. First there's the social situation in which a message is created and understood. Then there's the kind of relationship that's implied by the message itself, and that can be influenced by the form of the message.

Chapters 21–23 discuss different ways to take social context into consideration in your microstyle. Chapter 21 simply looks at the way micromessages, even written ones, evoke informal spoken conversation. Chapter 22 examines the way your communicative choices show how you think about your relationship with the person you're addressing. To sum it all up, Chapter 23 talks about how you can develop your own voice—a microvoice.

21

EVOKE CONVERSATION

One of the general lessons of this book is to relate your messages to people's real, everyday experience. One way to do that is to make reference to sensory experience. Another is to evoke the kinds of normal, intimate conversations that people have with their families, friends, and colleagues.

This technique is common in political slogans and company taglines. Eisenhower's campaign slogan I LIKE IKE, besides being a famous instance of poetic iconicity, is a striking example of the informal tone politicians use to try to connect with voters. Bill Clinton's campaign slogan IT'S THE ECONOMY, STUPID takes that informality all the way into the realm of intimate chiding.

Corporations often adopt an informal, conversational tone to try to sound like one of the gang. Amazon directly addresses its customer with its tagline . . . AND YOU'RE DONE. Sometimes companies presume to speak for their customers. Toyota puts words of admiration into our mouths with the slogan I LOVE WHAT YOU DO FOR ME. L'Oréal invites us to imagine each of its customers saying

BECAUSE I'M WORTH IT. Staples claims that a visit will leave us saying THAT WAS EASY. Even some company names directly address their customers, such as YouTube, or speak on their customers' behalf, such as MySpace or iLike, the "social music discovery service."

When messages sound conversational, the first questions that pop into my mind are, "Who is speaking?" and "Who is being addressed?" For some of the best slogans, these questions are hard to answer—or rather, they can be answered in different ways. The slogan IT'S THE ECONOMY, STUPID was not originally intended for voters. Rather, it was used to rally people working on Bill Clinton's 1992 campaign. In that context, it's possible to see the slogan as a self-deprecating phrase. If you were a campaign worker, you might say it to yourself while slapping yourself on the forehead, or you could imagine Bill Clinton saying it to himself. When the slogan gained popular traction, though, it seemed to taunt George H. W. Bush. It was innocent on the face of it, but it carried a barbed message.

A similarly ambiguous corporate slogan is Nike's JUST DO IT. This might be Nike telling you to get off your butt and go for a run. It could be you telling yourself the same thing. Or it could express the thoughts of an elite athlete trying to get a personal best or even break a world record. The phrase fits many different emotionally charged situations, and each one of those situations fits the Nike brand perfectly.

Think of all the movie titles that sound like they're plucked right out of an informal conversation:

ALICE DOESN'T LIVE HERE ANYMORE
DAMN YANKEES
DO THE RIGHT THING
GIMME SHELTER
GOODBYE, MR. CHIPS

MEET ME IN ST. LOUIS
SAY ANYTHING . . .
SHE'S GOTTA HAVE IT
HERE COMES MR. JORDAN

The following six-word memoir sums up a happy life story with a single conversational turn:

So far, so good; more please!
—*Richard May*, Smith Magazine, *February 5, 2008*

One of the *Onion*'s favorite techniques is to write headlines using the language of colloquial conversation. Here are some examples:

PEREGRINE FALCON ACTING PRETTY COCKY SINCE
BEING TAKEN OFF ENDANGERED SPECIES LIST

DEPT. OF HOMELAND SECURITY: "HAS ANYBODY
SEEN A BLUE FOLDER?"

GUY IN PHILOSOPHY CLASS NEEDS TO SHUT THE FUCK UP

By evoking a conversational context, a message draws on our actual experiences with people close to us and invites us to project an imaginary context in which we're hearing—or even uttering—the message. Women heard the L'Oréal slogan BECAUSE I'M WORTH IT while sitting in front of the TV, but they were expected to imagine a situation in which they would say that themselves—perhaps when a friend asked, "Why did you color your hair?"

When you evoke a conversational context, it's important to make it one that people would actually want to participate in. In the United Kingdom, push-up bra maker Wonderbra used the slogan HELLO BOYS. This is meant to be uttered by the woman wearing the bra—or perhaps even by the woman's breasts! It sounds like something a burlesque performer would say to her audience. Saucy, yes, but who talks like that anymore? And is that really the dream scenario for the customer?

Microstyle has its roots in everyday conversation. Its medium is informal language, and its success is determined by passing attention and memory in an environment where countless micromessages compete. What makes a micromessage successful is often the same thing that makes a comment stand out in a conversation: unusual perspicacity or wit. When you supplement conversation with a way to record and disseminate its highlights, you have a machine for cranking out microstyle.

The Vicious Circle (that's what the members of the Algonquin Round Table called their little club) was such a machine. The wit shown there was of the barbed variety (Groucho Marx, whose brother Harpo was a member, reportedly said about the group, "The price of admission is a serpent's tongue and a half-concealed stiletto"), but the basic dynamic of the group created a microcosm of microstyle. For a message to be successful, someone would have to think it memorable enough to recall after the conversation was over and interesting enough to be worth repeating. Now, for better or worse, social media make the whole world one big Vicious Circle.

22

ESTABLISH A RELATIONSHIP

"Sexting" is the sending of sexually explicit text and pic-
ture messages. It is not, apparently, an appropriate way to
submit a resume.

— @FakeAPStylebook, Twitter, February 18, 2010

Every act of communication implies a social relationship. In some languages, those relationships are explicitly reflected in grammar. If you're speaking French or German, you have to decide whether to use familiar or formal pronouns to address people. In Japanese, honorifics encode information about the relative status of speaker and addressee. Failure to use them properly can lead to social embarrassment.

English doesn't require us to make fundamental grammatical choices about social relationships, but what we say and the way we say it conveys a lot about how we understand an interaction and the relationship underlying it or implied by it. The effect can be as obvious as the difference between "Hey, dude" and "Excuse me, sir," but it can be considerably more subtle.

If you use social media, every message you send might begin a relationship (that's why we call them "social" media). Properties of the message set the tone for an interaction and can imply things about the relationship behind it. The implied relationship might be ad hoc, or intentional and long-standing. It might be friendly, professional, or even adversarial. But it's a relationship. Anything you say to someone provides clues about what you want your relationship to be like, or what you think it is like. Are you sharing professional information? Are you whispering asides to a confidante? Are you approaching a stranger for a favor?

Some kinds of messages are more conversational than others and make the implied relationship more obvious. Tweets, for example, very often have a conversational tone and are sometimes parts of actual conversations. Advertising and political slogans, while very different from tweets, often adopt a conversational tone, even though they aren't involved in the give-and-take of actual conversation. Even a company name can imply a relationship. Consider the name Yahoo!, and contrast it with a name like IBM. Yahoo! is something people might shout when they're excited. The relationship implied by Yahoo! isn't sober and professional. It's more like a crazy adventure that you're a part of. That's really pretty appropriate for a web portal and directory. Yahoo! was one of the first big web companies; when it started out, the web *was* a big adventure.

After the financial collapse of 2008, WaMu (a bank previously known as Washington Mutual) failed and was bought by Chase. Chase swaggered into town with an aggressive ad campaign— you could see its slogans all over the city on buses. Here's one of those slogans:

LET'S START BANKING BETTER, WASHINGTON

What a disaster of relationship building! I'm sure Chase intended this as kind of an upbeat, inclusive rallying cry. Instead, it sounded like a parent scolding a child. Not good for a megabank waltzing in from the East Coast trying to set things right in this green little corner of the nation.

Negotiating a relationship means establishing the context in which your communication is meant to take place. Is it at work, with family, or with friends? Products are often naturally aligned with one such life context, and that determines a lot about how they get advertised. Beer, for example, is typically consumed by men in informal social situations, so the messages in beer ads are fashioned for that context. Redhook beer, for example, used the following slogan on a billboard I spotted in Seattle:

REDHOOK THINKS YOUR BOSS IS A RAVING LUNATIC TOO

This message explicitly sets itself up in opposition to a professional context. With it, Redhook is adopting the persona of a peer expressing solidarity with a downtrodden employee. The presupposition of the message, that the reader has a boss and believes that person to be a raving lunatic, implies that the experience is universal. Reading this message is supposed to make you feel like one of the guys. Similarly, the slogan WE'LL LEAVE A LIGHT ON FOR YOU casts Motel 6 as your family, awaiting your safe arrival home.

You can get some laughs with a micromessage by toying with relationships. A great example is this bumper sticker:

JESUS LOVES YOU. (EVERYONE ELSE THINKS
YOU'RE AN ASSHOLE.)

"Jesus loves you" is a blessing typically offered by a Christian believer to the world in general. The insulting addendum here, however, makes us reimagine that familiar relationship in different ways. One possibility is that the speaker is actually a Christian simultaneously sharing Jesus's love and dishing out nasty insults. A more likely possibility, perhaps, is that the speaker isn't a Christian at all, but is addressing Christians. People who say "Jesus loves you" indiscriminately might feel that they're being kind, but in fact they're trumpeting their beliefs in a way that might be considered presumptuous by Jews, Muslims, Hindus, atheists, and other non-Christians. They are, in a sense, talking to themselves—preaching to the choir. So another implication of the parenthetical in the bumper sticker is that the person laying claim to Jesus's love is acting like a jerk.

Applying the "wrong" relationship to a message can be funny. Here's a tweet from @Apelad that appeared in the book *Twitter Wit*:

All 7-year-olds have good hustle.

There's something delightfully ridiculous about discussing kids in general as if you're a coach evaluating athletes. Another bit of *Twitter Wit* comments on the tweeter's expectations of Twitter messages:

Thanks for heightening my understanding of the Arab-Israeli conflict with your inappropriately serious status updates.
— *@Someecards*

Movie titles like *It Happened One Night* and *Once Upon a Time in America* clearly establish a storyteller-audience relationship. Titles like the second one that allude to fairy tales complicate matters by implying that the audience is composed of children. Like all such indirect associations, this one should be viewed skeptically, but it does invite people to approach the movie with a sort of childlike wonder.

SOCIAL MEDIA

Establishing relationships in the age of social media is tough, but important. Twitter, in particular, is a bizarre combination of professional self-presentation and personal extroversion. Some people actually use Twitter in an official professional capacity; some have been hired to be the social media voice of a large corporation, for example. Avid users are on it all day, whether they're working or playing. When working, they sometimes use it in a quasi-professional way, asking technical questions, doing brief, informal market surveys, and so on. Other times they use it more like the watercooler, to kvetch about their jobs and their clients, discuss the news, gossip about celebrities, and otherwise engage in screen-mediated chitchat. Social norms about what is expected or appropriate on Twitter haven't really jelled yet, and probably never will—not, at least, before Twitter gives way to a new platform for communication.

If there's any shared expectation about communicating with social media, it's that people will be "honest" and "real." That's supposed to distinguish social media from old-fashioned one-way publication and broadcasting. But how honest is too honest, and how real is too real? Any one of those little creations you've let loose in the digital wilderness might come back to haunt you. If you make a self-deprecating remark, will a future employer or client see it and be put off? Will they appreciate your openness as much as the true Twitterati do?

People have already begun to declare themselves social media experts, and many warn about the perils of oversharing and of undersharing. These expressions can refer to both the quality and the quantity of a person's tweets. Oversharing means posting too often, posting messages that are too personal, or posting messages that are just too banal. Undersharing means not using Twitter often enough or just not being forthcoming enough. How can we know when we're oversharing? What are the boundaries in a relationship that's not real and that takes place in a realm where all barriers between the personal and the professional have come down? These are questions we all have to work out together.

23

CREATE A MICROVOICE

Only use "weekend" as a verb when you wish to let readers know you're some kind of fancy boy.
— @FAKEAPSTYLEBOOK, Twitter, March 15, 2010

In his book *You Are Not a Gadget,* Jaron Lanier argues that the collectivist ethos of the web obscures the voice of the individual. On websites like Wikipedia, contributions are for the most part anonymous and can be edited and deleted by anyone. What remains is a text often authored by committee. Sites like Twitter are a more complicated case. While the main value of Twitter derives from an aggregate of voices rather than the strength of any one voice, it still provides a forum for the individual voice in a miniature form. Some people gain followers simply by sharing popular links and news items, but others make quips and observations and otherwise use microstyle to create a microvoice.

To participate in the web conversation, it's crucial to use language to create a voice. When you add a comment to a blog or contribute to an online forum, unless you're a familiar contributor with a reputation, you'll be making a personal impression based entirely on your use of language.

That's one reason why, when online conversations degenerate into flame wars, few issues throw off quite as much heat as the spelling, punctuation, and grammar of the participants. This is partly just an expression of the pop prescriptivism that I discussed in the introduction, but there's more going on. The online obsession with grammar and style might be a sign of the deep anxiety about communication that the web creates. When we "converse" with people through forums and blog comment sections, we often know little about them beyond what they convey through their text. That means the text makes an easy target, but it also means we really don't know who we're dealing with—is it someone whose opinion counts, or just some jerk? When our ideas are criticized without an institutional framework to confer authority and without the rich real-world social connections that reassure us about people's intentions, we feel vulnerable. We seize on whatever we can to establish identity and negotiate social roles.

These difficulties posed by social media and the web point to the importance of creating a microvoice.

Advertisers have been working on the problem of the microvoice for decades, though they have both the advantage and the disadvantage of a more rigidly defined relationship within which to do so. People know what to expect from companies trying to sell them products. Nevertheless, a wide range of options are available to advertisers.

A certain type of ad slogan—one that seems quaint now— uses formal, labored language to create an authoritative voice. For example, in the 1950s Buick used the endless slogan TODAY THE DISCRIMINATING FAMILY FINDS IT ABSOLUTELY NECESSARY TO OWN TWO OR MORE MOTOR CARS. The appeal to a mythical "discriminating" family, one with high status and taste, gives Buick customers a role model to emulate while buying cars willy-nilly. The language used to make that appeal has the stilted formality that consumers might expect from members of such a family. A similar slogan is Cadillac's 1961 THE NEW CADILLAC IS SO PRACTICAL TO OWN AND SO ECONOMICAL TO OPERATE THAT IT IS ACKNOWLEDGED MOTORDOM'S WISEST INVESTMENT.

Nowadays a slogan is likely to be extremely informal and even irreverent, like the tagline for Biznik: BUSINESS NETWORKING THAT DOESN'T SUCK. According to one of the cofounders, this tagline is off-putting to some older and more conservative customers, but it rings true to the younger and more "alternative" crowd that Biznik targets.

Notice that the title of this chapter is not "Use Your Own Voice." Though that's certainly a fine thing to do. You can use any voice you want to, as long as it's one you control and one that works. Voice seems mysterious, but it's really not. Voice is what the recipient of your message infers about you solely from your communicative choices. It's a matter of what you say and the specific words and constructions you use to say it. A voice implies an attitude or even a whole persona—a fictitious character or projected personal image that might correspond only imperfectly, or not at all, with who you really are. As the oft-quoted caption from a *New Yorker* cartoon put it, "On the Internet, nobody knows you're a dog." You can be anyone you want, as long as you can use a voice convincingly.

When I write my blog, The Name Inspector, I adopt a persona that's a sort of cartoon version of myself. It highlights certain aspects of my training and experience and a certain side of my sense of humor. I always refer to "The Name Inspector" in the third person, distancing myself from the persona and poking a little fun at the authority he claims. It's amazing how disarming this strategy can be. People find authority and advice more palatable when they're presented in cartoon form. It's kind of a game, and people recognize that and play along. I often get email with salutations such as "Dear Mr. Inspector."

A failure of voice can result from a lack of consistency in attitude or style. Consider the ad campaign for Microsoft's Hotmail. It features the tagline TOOLS FOR THE NEW BUSY and uses a number of different slogans to characterize what is meant by "the new busy." But the slogans are all over the map. Some sound suspiciously like the old busy:

MAKE BEAVERS LOOK LAZY

LIKE TO PLAY "FILL THE CALENDAR"

WOULD BE OPEN TO TAKING A CLASS IN THEIR SLEEP

THINK 9 TO 5 IS A CUTE IDEA

Others declare independence from the old busy:

ARE NOT LIKE THE OLD BUSY

ARE NOT THE TOO BUSY

Still others are just confusing:

LOOK FOR INTERESTING WAYS TO BE BORED

(What does this even mean? And how is looking for a way to be bored consistent with the idea of being busy in a new, exciting way?)

MIGHT TELL YOU THEIR SECRET SAUCE RECIPE

(What does this have to do with being busy?)

Voice is hard to create with a single micromessage, but not impossible. Micromessages can subtly include or exclude. Ragu uses the slogan FEED OUR KIDS WELL, which has a very odd combination of an imperative form and a first person plural possessive form in the phrase "our kids." The implication is that all children belong to everyone, and that we all have a responsibility to take care of them. It's an "it takes a village" sentiment. Yet the responsibility is on *you*.

Different words and phrases belong to different *registers*: some we use informally among friends, and others we use while making formal presentations to colleagues. The type of language you use helps set the tone for a conversation and establish your role as a participant. When a company introduces itself with its name, its tagline, and its other marketing material, it can use register to place itself in a particular social role. It might play the part of a respected authority, a friendly colleague, or a subservient helper.

In the 1990s there was a fad for pseudo-Latin names like Agilent, Lucent, Cingular, and Aptiva. Web businesses in both the original dot-com boom and the Web 2.0 period have given us whimsy in names like Google, Yahoo!, Twitter, and Squidoo. These are opposing strategies for defining roles. The Latin lovers present themselves as authority figures who are associated with learned fields such as law and science and are therefore worthy of our trust. But a name like Yahoo! is definitely not trying to establish authority. It presents a company not as an authority figure but as a smart, savvy peer, and it initiates an informal and fun interaction.

Using a voice unconvincingly can make you look foolish. Dr. Scholl's uses the following slogan for Massaging Gel shoe insoles: ARE YOU GELLIN'? This seems to be an allusion to *chillin'*, which makes it an embarrassing misappropriation of "hip" slang to sell an old person's product. The result is funny, and it's not clear that it's supposed to be. Pillsbury used the slogan NOTHIN' SAYS LOVIN' LIKE SOMETHIN' FROM THE OVEN, which sounds like a bad line from a lascivious soul tune about muffins.

The most important role you inhabit might still be your own

voice. If you don't, somebody else will. One of the most unsavory aspects of the social media boom has been the eagerness with which some companies want to speak on your behalf. It's never been easier to announce something to the whole world without even knowing it. Who hasn't had the embarrassing experience of signing up for a new online service only to find that you've inadvertently spammed your whole contact list by failing to deselect a checkbox? Or that you've posted to Twitter to let everyone know you've signed up?

In early 2010, Seattle tech journalist John Cook wrote about a company called HelpHive that was placing ads for local businesses on Craigslist, unbeknownst to the businesses in question. The ads didn't link to the companies' websites, but to companies' profiles on the HelpHive website. John Surdi, the owner of Crystal Carpet Cleaning & Restoration, and one of the beneficiaries of this unsolicited help, said, "I am concerned. I really don't want people writing my ad copy."

Many web services connected to Twitter will automatically generate a Tweet, written in the first person and sent from your Twitter account, announcing something like, "I just signed up for _____!" Facebook users sometimes find that they've "invited" all their contacts to use an app along with them. For a while, Facebook itself was turning its users into unwitting stars of online ads with its Beacon program (which was killed after the protestations of Facebook's users).

These presumptuous ad programs are just one more way in which the problems of celebrity have become the problems of everyone. Laws dating from the 1890s protect individuals from having their likenesses used without permission in advertising. These laws were designed to protect famous people, but now they're being invoked on behalf of regular people.

The ease with which you can publish with social media has this darker side: it's easy for others to publish words in your name, literally speaking in your voice. As in other areas of life, the cost of convenience is a loss of control. The more we rely on tools to automate our online communications, the easier it becomes for others to commandeer our voices. If you want to maintain the integrity of your online presence, it's important to be in control of your own voice. Or voices. Even if you use different personae online, it's important to be in control of each one. Cultivating and controlling your own voice online isn't just good "personal branding." It's an assertion of freedom.

EPILOGUE

In this book I've tried to reveal the color and richness of the little verbal messages that bombard us all. I think about microstyle every day when I work with my naming and verbal branding clients, but I've realized it has a deeper importance that goes beyond its practical applications. Microstyle is the basis for everyday verbal creativity, the poetics of the vernacular. Paying attention to microstyle can help you establish a more positive relationship with language, one based on the appreciation of what works, not on insecurity about what's right and wrong.

Microstyle was once for specialists, but now it's for everyone. That change was created by social media, but now it's simply part of our verbal culture. The era of microstyle isn't about technology; it's about a new dynamics of verbal communication that technology happened to make possible. We're not going backward, and microstyle isn't going away. So why not make an effort to pay attention to it? Keep a notebook where you record interesting slogans, headlines, tweets, sound bites, and other micromessages you come across. Collect examples of the different tools described in this book. Try out some of the tools in the messages you produce yourself. A tweet, or even an email subject line, can always be improved by an apt metaphor, a vivid image, or a poetic sound.

Microstyle is interesting because it's an expression of often-unstudied verbal creativity. Some of the most revealing forms of microstyle might be the ones people produce when they don't think anyone's listening. When people sit down and type phrases into Google, they're talking about *what they want*. Google isn't God, but web searches are often like prayers. That's what prompted John Battelle, who wrote a book about Google called *The Search*, to coin the term "the database of intentions." In that book he speculated about the perfect search engine:

> *Imagine the ability to ask any question and get not just an accurate answer, but your perfect answer—an answer that suits the context and intent of your question, an answer that with eerie precision is informed by who you are and why you're asking.*

Of course, it's just as likely that we'll receive inaccurate answers, misleading answers, that are otherwise just as precise and perfect. The web has created the possibility for a whole economy based on hypothetical things rather than real things. People type their desires into search engines. Search engine optimization specialists and advertisers conduct research on what the most popular web searches are. People who register domains just to publish pay-per-click ads on them capture traffic with phrases that people frequently use in their web searches.

During the original dot-com bubble, generic domain names became absurdly expensive. The coveted domains were the ones, like pets.com, that corresponded to existing industries with large markets. But web marketers now invest in phrase domains like dateaceleb.com, some of which correspond to existing businesses, but many of which correspond merely to hypothetical businesses that people might *wish* existed. So the web provides a complete system for collecting and exploiting people's desires. As long as people profit from our tiniest acts of attention on the web, they'll be driven to capture that attention in any way they can. That includes dangling before us phrases that describe seductive hypothetical ideas, that name and sometimes even create our desires without leading to any satisfaction of them.

But where there's an opportunity to take advantage, there's also an opportunity to meet a need. There's actually a company, called Domain Strategies, whose business model is to buy great domain names and build real businesses around them. The name comes first, and the business comes after. Domain Strategies owns the name dateaceleb.com. So maybe I'll actually be able to have dinner with Tina Fey someday, if my wife lets me.

ACKNOWLEDGMENTS

It would be fun to say that the wild success of my blog The Name Inspector had publishers clamoring to offer me a lucrative book contract. But in fact, my blog has a modest but loyal readership, and this book came about the old-fashioned way. I struggled through versions of a book proposal until I got one right, and was escorted through the process with patience and savvy by my wonderful agent Lisa DiMona of Lark Productions. This book wouldn't have happened without her. Superprolific marketing guru Seth Godin, who is also her client, generously referred me to her when I approached him for help, and I thank him.

I should also thank two editors from other presses who were especially generous with their comments on my proposal: Emily Loose of Free Press, and Marty Asher of Knopf.

Brendan Curry was the one editor who really saw the potential in my proposal and ran with it. I thank him for championing my book at W. W. Norton & Company, and for making such great and detailed editorial comments on the manuscript. And I thank everyone up the line at Norton for giving the project the thumbs-up. My copy editor, Stephanie Hiebert, did an amazing job tightening up the writing, tracking down facts, and generally making the book seem finished.

I also have to thank all the awesome baristas at three Seattle cafés—Victrola Coffee and Art on 15th Avenue, Elliott Bay Café, and Oddfellows—for giving me my offices-away-from-home. They never looked at me funny for sitting there all day, they were nice when my kids came in with me, and most important, they make a good cup of coffee. And I *really* like coffee. And I thank the Helen Rabinoff Whiteley Center for allowing me to stay in the most amazing little cottage on San Juan Island to concentrate solely on my book for a week. Calling these places cottages doesn't do them justice—they're completely modern and comfortable, with full kitchens and gas fireplaces, they're beautifully designed, and they sit in utterly peaceful and quiet woods overlooking Friday Harbor. I also thank the Washington Center for the Book for letting me use the Eulalie and Carlos Scandiuzzi Writers' Room at the main branch of the Seattle Public Library. This is a comfortable and quiet space at the top of a really cool building designed by Rem Koolhaas.

I'd like to thank my Twitter friends Nancy Friedman (@Fritinancy) and James Callan (@scarequotes) for being entertaining and supportive.

Fred Zimmerman, my oldest friend in the world, discussed my book idea with me from the earliest stages. Come to think of it, my interest in microstyle dates back to our postcollege days, when he and I made up names for a magazine that we never started. My favorite was "The Respectable Bespectacled Spectator."

Thanks to Tony Hacker for helping me keep things in perspective.

And now for the people who really got me through this, day in and day out: my family. My mother-in-law Shellie Bailkin came through with crucial child care when we really needed it. My sons Tobias (6) and Finn (3), who are hilarious and give great hugs, always reminded me how to feel relaxed and happy when I was stressed out, and vice versa. And my wife, Jordanna Bailkin— what can I say about her? She's funny, fearless, brilliant, beautiful, and an old hand at this book-writing stuff. She takes good care of me, gives me delicious treats, and delivers a hell of a pep talk.

INDEX